KITTEN AND CAT CARE

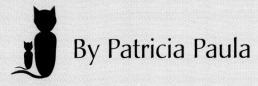

By Patricia Paula

With millions of cat-owning households throughout the world, it is apparent that cats continue to remain one of the most popular domestic pets. At first glance, some people become enamored of cats simply because of the qualities that are unique to felines, such as their independent nature, their gracefulness, and their overall beauty. While this is indeed true, cats have other qualities that recommend them as pets: they can live comfortably in the smallest of apartments, they do not have to be walked, and they can easily keep themselves amused when their human family is not at home.

With life-long owner commitment and the right care, your cat can be a happy, healthy pet and companion...and that's what this publication is all about.

The Publisher would like to acknowledge the owners of the cats pictured in this book: Sandra Adler, Bob Balas, M. Baum, Richard & Lori Bilello, Mr. & Mrs. D. Boyce, Kim Brantley, M. Caiazza, Kaye Chambers, Donna Chandler, Kathleen Comstock, M. Conoe, Annie Courdille, M. Danielou, Pat & David Dannenberg, Sheila Dentico, Valerie Anne Edwards, M. Enesman, Alice L. Faber, M. Ferenczi, Susan Ferguson, M. Gagnon, Richard Gebhardt, Meredith Gowell, Isobel Graff, Alain Guillerme, Vickie L. Hansen, Ruth Hodges, Holiday Cattery, M. Host, A. & J. Huemmer, K. Huemmer, Karen Jacobus, Java Cats, M. Kalt, Cher Kelly, Margaret Lowther, Sal Maniace, Jr., Vicky Markstein, Donna McDonald, John McGonagle, Laura M. Moody, Mary Morea, Michael E. Nelson, Sharon & Anthony Pestano, Charmayne Phillips, Doris-Cttinn Reese, Jose Reyes, Sally K. Robison, Carol Rothfeld, Caroline Scott, Allen Scruggs, June Shatto, Bonnie L. Smith, Jane Stiner, Linda Swierczynski, B. Tanner, Joan Tellier, Bob & Linda Thaler, Michael Tucker, Norma Volpe, Mary Von Paulus, Carol Decker White, and M. Zaire.

Photography: Glen Axelrod, Isabelle Francais, and Robert Pearcy.

What are Quarterlies?

Books, the usual way information of this sort is transmitted, can be too slow. Sometimes by the time a book is written and published, the material contained therein is a year or two old...and no new material has been added during that time. Only a book in a magazine form can bring breaking stories and current information. A magazine is streamlined in production, so we have adopted certain magazine publishing techniques in the creation of this Cat Quarterly. Magazines also can be much cheaper than books because they are supported by advertising. To combine these assets into a great publication, we issued this Quarterly in both magazine and book format at different prices.

yearBOOKS,INC.
Dr. Herbert R. Axelrod,
Founder & Chairman

Neal Pronek
Chief Editor

yearBOOKS are all photo composed, color separated and designed on Scitex equipment in Neptune, N.J. with the following staff:

DIGITAL PRE-PRESS
Patricia Northrup
Supervisor

Robert Onyrscuk
Jose Reyes

COMPUTER ART
Patti Escabi
Sandra Taylor Gale
Candida Moreira
Joanne Muzyka
Francine Shulman

ADVERTISING SALES
George Campbell
National Advertising Manager
Amy Manning
Advertising Director
Sandy Cutillo
Advertising Coordinator
Nancy Rivadeneira
Periodicals Advertising Sales Manager
Cheryl Blyth
Periodicals Sales Representative

©yearBOOKS, Inc.
1 TFH Plaza
Neptune, N.J. 07753
Completely manufactured in Neptune, N.J.
USA

Designed by Candida Moreira
Cover design by Sherise Buhagiar

CATS QUARTERLY

Distributed in the UNITED STATES to the Pet Trade by T.F.H. Publications, Inc., One T.F.H. Plaza, Neptune City, NJ 07753; in CANADA Rolf C. Hagen Inc., 3225 Sartelon St. Laurent-Montreal Quebec H4R 1E8; Pet Trade by H & L Pet Supplies Inc., 27 Kingston Crescent, Kitchener, Ontario N2B 2T6; in ENGLAND by T.F.H. Publications, PO Box 15, Waterlooville PO7 6BQ; in AUSTRALIA AND THE SOUTH PACIFIC by T.F.H. (Australia), Pty. Ltd., Box 149, Brookvale 2100 N.S.W., Australia; in NEW ZEALAND by Brooklands Aquarium Ltd. 5 McGiven Drive, New Plymouth, RD1 New Zealand; in SOUTH AFRICA, Rolf C. Hagen S.A. (PTY.) LTD. P.O. Box 201199, Durban North 4016, South Africa; in Japan by T.F.H. Publications, Japan—Jiro Tsuda, 10-12-3 Ohjidai, Sakura, Chiba 285, Japan. Published by T.F.H. Publications, Inc.

MANUFACTURED IN THE
UNITED STATES OF AMERICA
BY T.F.H. PUBLICATIONS, INC.

USA 22

Siamese Cat, Exotic Shorthair Cat

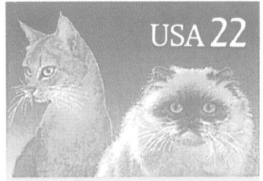

USA 22

Abyssinian Cat, Himalayan Cat

USA 22

Maine Coon Cat, Burmese Cat

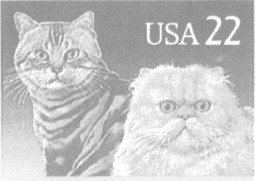

USA 22

American Shorthair Cat, Persian Cat

USA 22

Siamese Cat, Exotic Shorthair Cat

USA 22

Abyssinian Cat, Himalayan Cat

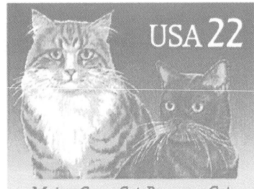

USA 22

Maine Coon Cat, Burmese Cat

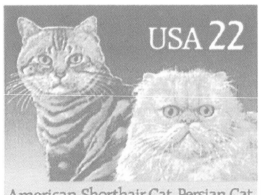

USA 22

American Shorthair Cat, Persian Cat

Commemorative cat stamps issued in the 1980s.

CONTENTS

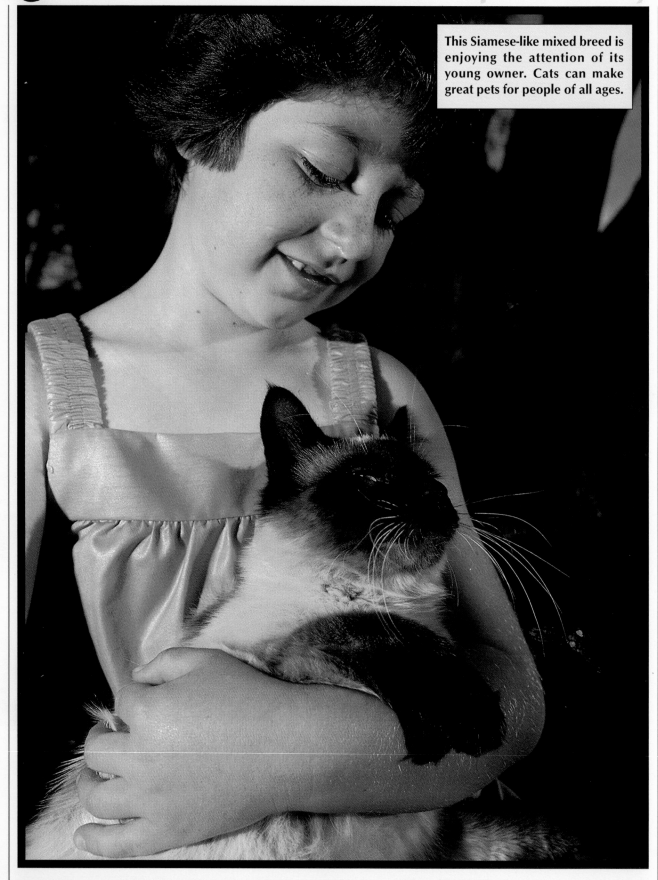

This Siamese-like mixed breed is enjoying the attention of its young owner. Cats can make great pets for people of all ages.

THE CAT AS A PET

The fact that you have picked up this book on domestic cats and kittens would indicate that you are interested in finding out a little more about these elegant members of the family Felidae. You are not alone. At this time, cats and kittens have become one of the most desirable of all pets. Everyone is familiar with the cat; it is, after all, a very common pet and can be seen roaming the alleys and streets of most large cities. Why then has it suddenly become so desirable? In a nutshell, the answer to this question is the fact that it is the most convenient of all the pets from which you can choose.

This is the starting point; but, once acquired, people soon begin to appreciate the numerous virtues of these individualistic predators. They are sensitive creatures born of a few hundred generations of animals that have had a very mixed relationship with us humans. Totally different from the dog in their attitude to life, they pay homage to no one, including their owner. They are essentially loners that will happily share your home with you on a mutually workable basis. For your part, you will provide their food, see that they are nicely groomed, and provide a warm, comfy place for them to sleep. If they become ill, you will see that they receive the correct veterinary treatment, and of course you will allow them the total freedom of your house. For their part, they will favor you by staying to enjoy these benefits! This is the cat.

Now you may think that this seems a pretty one-sided arrangement, but this is why the cat is such a sophisticated pet. If you do not live up to your part, then do not expect your cat to be around too long: it will sooner or later

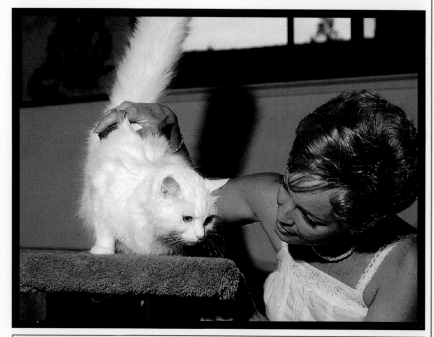

Some cats are more responsive to people than are others; some will have a favorite person among the members of their human family.

find someone else more appreciative of its presence. If not, it will return to the wild side and look after its own welfare, something cats have been doing very well throughout their evolution.

The very independent nature of the cat is the basis of its sheer convenience. You will not need to take it for a walk, for roaming around the house is more than enough exercise. It will not go out terrorizing the neighborhood as might a large dog left to its own devices, nor will it howl and bark when left at home. Cats like being indoors, and there's far fewer dangers in your home than there are outdoors.

You will not need an array of expensive equipment to own a cat as you would if you decided to keep tropical fish, nor will you need to reduce the pet to a virtual prisoner by caging it as you would with rabbits, guinea pigs, hamsters, or birds. In the cat, you have a pet that can be given total freedom, yet will happily stay with you, and at the same time not be regarded as a nuisance or a threat to other people in your neighborhood.

Your kitten, and the cat it grows up to become, will not cost you a fortune to feed, its housing needs are simplicity itself. Even the cost of the kitten need not be more than a modest sum if you decide to own a non-purebred. If you give your kitten a great deal of affection, this will be returned in kind. It will happily curl up on your lap and purr contentedly. It will amuse you with its antics and its superb jumping and acrobatic abilities. A kitten really is the most comical of pets and it finds pleasure in the simplest of articles to play with.

own thing. It is impossible to say which sort of cat you will acquire because they are not as predictable as dogs. They are harder to fathom at times, yet this is part of their appeal. Some are very lazy, others very active. For these reasons, once hooked on them, most owners will end up with two or more felines.

With a cat and a kitten, what you see is what you get. While a little puppy may grow up to be a veritable giant, this will never happen with your kitten. All cats stay within very tolerable size limits, so, from a management viewpoint, you

you will have more than enough to choose from. You can also have a kitten in one of a number of fur types: long, medium, short, curly, or, if the unusual appeals to you, even one with virtually no hair. Most cats have a long tail, but there are breeds with short tails, and one that may have no tail at all. There two breeds with unusual ears, one having them folded and the other with curled ears. However, it is best to select from cats that are essentially as nature intended them to be; this, after all, ensures that they

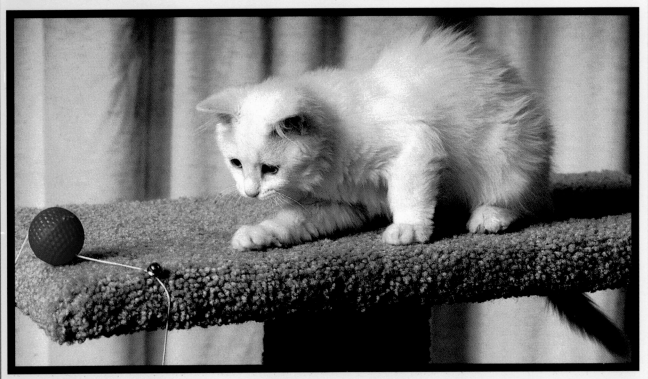

You will find that when a cat moves in, most sensible mice move out, so there is a practical benefit in owning a cat. Some cats will follow you around your home, constantly seeking your attention and always wanting to be with you. Some will enjoy walking with you around your garden; others will prefer to do their

A scratching post and toys are a must for every cat-owning household.

are assured that your kitten will not grow to a size that you did not anticipate.

The potential range of color and coat pattern combinations in cats is enormous, so

will be less prone to health problems.

If the idea of breeding and exhibiting cats appeals to you, then you will find there is a large and well-established hobby based upon just this aspect. Indeed, the hobby has grown to such an extent that there are a few people who make a full-time living from

American Shorthair kittens. The distinctive markings above the eyes are characteristic of the breed.

Youngsters should be taught early on about how to properly handle the family cat. Caring for a pet can help to teach a child a sense of responsibility.

breeding and showing their stock. However, working up to such a level is a costly and time-consuming business. Most breeders and exhibitors involve themselves purely as a pastime.

Although cats are essentially loners when out and about, they are nonetheless far more social than was thought for many years. This so, they will certainly enjoy

apartment and house renters, forbid the owning of dogs, they will accept cats. This reflects the unobtrusive and quiet nature of these stealthy animals. Given all the virtues of cats and kittens, you may be wondering if they have any faults. It would be misleading to say they are all angels. Many will catch and kill most rodents from mice to squirrels, and they will not shy

life. You cannot train them as you can a dog, so don't expect them to come to your bid and call like some benign servant. They will come if they feel so disposed, and generally they will if they are in a loving home, and especially at meal times! Kittens are easy to litter train, and providing they have access to a scratching post they will not damage your furniture. They certainly

Lilac Siamese and blue cream Balinese. In essence, the Balinese is a Siamese in a longhaired coat.

the company of their own kind in your home. I would say without hesitation that if you are thinking of having a kitten, you cannot go wrong by having two. They are little more trouble to look after and will provide you with a constant source of companionship and amusement.

You will find that while many government housing projects, as well as many

away from bringing these home to you, along with any birds that they can pounce on. This predatory aspect of their nature may not appeal to every person, but with such a born hunter it is a fact of

will not bite pieces out of it as dogs may sometimes do if not trained.

With a cat, you have the rare opportunity of having in your home a lion or leopard in miniature. This is an animal that is only partially domesticated in many instances. It can as easily return to the wild and survive as it can settle for a more comfortable existence in your company.

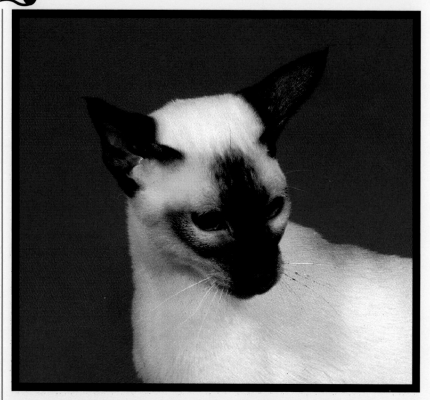

Top: The Siamese is one of the most popular breeds in the cat fancy. The points—face mask, ears, paws, and tail—come in four different colors: chocolate, blue, lilac, and seal, which is shown here. Bottom: American Bobtail. This cat is a relative newcomer among the bobtailed breeds. It is known for its lively, intelligent personality.

There are not many pets that this can be said of. Whether for the young, or the more elderly, kittens and cats are truly adorable pets that will fit in with your daily routine with no problem at all. They make few demands on you and actually offer a great deal in return.

If you already own a dog, a rabbit, or other pets larger, or almost as large as a cat, then you will find that a feline will quickly become a friend to them, the more so if you obtain a kitten. Throughout this introduction to the cat, you will note that I have stressed that it is a more convenient pet than any other popular animal. This does not suggest it is a better pet than a dog or a parrot, because such judgments, of necessity, can only be determined on a personal basis. If you are looking for a pet that can live in your home, that will be an affectionate companion, yet will not be intrusive by its presence, then a cat a is very good choice.

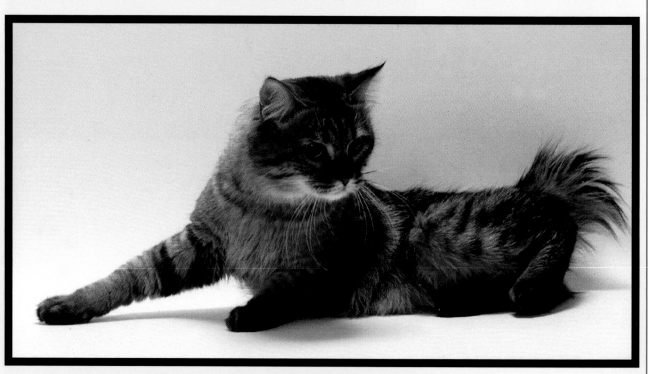

WHAT WILL THE CAT NEED?

One of the considerable advantages in owning a cat is the fact that there are actually very few items that are needed in order to care for it in a home environment. A number of them could be supplied from items you probably have in the house already. This said, most owners will prefer to purchase at least some basic articles specifically for their new companion. The range of equipment made for cats is extensive. Here we can review some of those that will be needed in one form or another.

CAT CARRIER

This is an item that often proves extremely handy over the years. It is needed when taking the cat to the vet, or when there is a need to confine it, or when a home move is in the cards. It is essential if you like to take the kitten or cat on vacation with you. If you decide to exhibit your cats, then of course it is mandatory that one or more cat carriers are owned. Be sure that the one chosen will be large enough for the adult cat; otherwise, you will have to purchase another one at a later date.

It should be strong, well supplied with ventilation holes, and have a secure means of fastening it. If you are likely to travel a lot, then do invest in the biggest and best one that you can find.

SCRATCHING POST

In order to remove the possibility of the cat scratching your furniture, it is best

A cat travel bag will enable you to transport your cat safely and comfortably. Photo courtesy of Sherpa's Pet Trading Company.

to obtain a good scratching post. This may be a freestanding unit, or one which is screwed to the wall. Pet shops stock a variety of scratching posts. A lightweight ball attached to a piece of string can be suspended from the top of the post. This will encourage the kitten to play, and thus use the post.

LITTER TRAY

Cats are extremely clean pets and will foul your home only if they have no means of doing otherwise. A litter tray is essential for a kitten, which cannot control its bowel movements for more than a few seconds. Plastic trays are available from your pet shop. Purchase the larger ones, ideally those with raised removable sides that will prevent the litter from being

scattered over the floor. Initially, this add-on piece may not be needed because the kitten will be small. It is useful as kitty becomes a cat—especially with those who take the job of covering fecal matter extremely seriously and spend ages attending to this. You can purchase igloo types, which have a covered top which reduces, or restricts, the odors created. However, most of the better brands of cat litter are impregnated with an odor absorber. You will need a plastic scoop to remove litter and fecal matter, because cats do not like to use an already fouled tray. If it is not kept clean, this will merely discourage the cat from using it; thus it may be forced to attend to its toiletry needs elsewhere in the house.

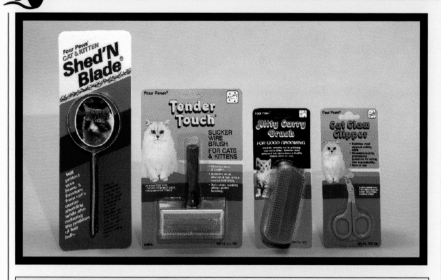

Your cat should be groomed on a regular basis. From brushes to nail clippers, your pet shop will meet your pet's every grooming need. Photo courtesy of Four Paws.

FOOD AND WATER DISHES

There is a wide selection of dishes, mostly in plastic, that can be obtained for cats. Earthenware (crock) and aluminum are more costly but longer lasting. You could use saucers for the food, and these are actually as good as any special dishes because you are not likely to be tempted to pile too much food onto them. This is better because cats are ideally fed little and often, rather than having a dish full which they will not always eat, and which will thus attract flies and start to go dry.

CAT COLLAR AND ID TAG

Collars for cats must be elasticized to reduce the risk of the kitten or cat becoming caught up on a branch when it is out and about. The ID tag, which should bear your name, address, and phone number, is an obvious need in case the cat gets lost. Some collars have bells fitted to them so it is not as easy for the cat to catch mice, birds and the like. However, these

Right: Lilac point Birman. Regular grooming is especially important with the longhaired breeds. In addition to keeping your cat looking its best, it can help to prevent skin and coat problems. Below: This stylish scratching post features several perches, as well as an enclosure at the bottom.

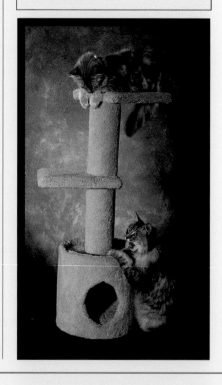

are not successful if the cat is a skilled hunter.

If you plan to take your kitten with you on vacation, or short trips, you might consider the purchase of a cat harness, additional to its collar. It must be made for cats and not small dogs. Most are of a nylon material so they are very light. The harness gives you a little more control over the cat in the event that it is startled and attempts to back out of its collar. Cats do not like walking on a collar/harness and lead but some, especially those of foreign type, take to it more readily, particularly if they are trained to this from kittenhood.

GROOMING AIDS

The grooming tools that you will need for your kitten will be determined by its coat length. Shorthaired cats require only a brush and a medium/fine toothed comb. For longhaired breeds, you may find the double-sided brush with pins on one side and bristles on the other a useful addition. You can also purchase rubber curry-type combs that are not as severe on the coat as those with wire pins. Bristle brushes and steel combs are preferred to plastic, as the latter creates a lot of static electricity in longhaired coats. A pair of curved and blunt-ended scissors may also be useful

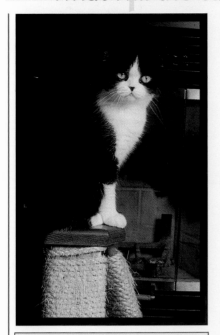

Scratching posts come in a variety of styles and sizes. There is one to fit every budget.

for tidying up the long hairs on the feet of longhaired breeds.

CAT BEDS

There is a good choice of cat beds available for cats. They are made of wicker, plastic, canvas, wood, or fiberglass. The chosen bed should be easy to clean, which makes fiberglass an excellent choice. Although some cats will use a bed, most chose not to. They would much rather curl up on the sofa, a nice chair, or your bed. They prefer to be off of the floor most of the time when they go to sleep, so if you do purchase a bed, try to put it in an elevated area.

TOYS AND OTHER ITEMS

Your local pet store will have a wide range of cat toys from which you can choose. The more sophisticated and expensive playthings, such as climbing frames covered in carpeting, will provide a lot of enjoyment for kittens and cats—the more so if they have things dangling from them. Cats like to paw at these kinds of toys.

You can purchase such things as playpens, or heating pads for the kitty's bed, but these items are not at all necessary. A much better investment would be to purchase a few specialty books on cats and subjects related to them—maybe one devoted to the particular breed you decide to own. It is always wise to obtain as many of the desired accessories as you can in advance of the arrival day of the kitten or cat. This way, you have more chance to shop around and to be sure everything is on hand when the kitten is eventually introduced to the household.

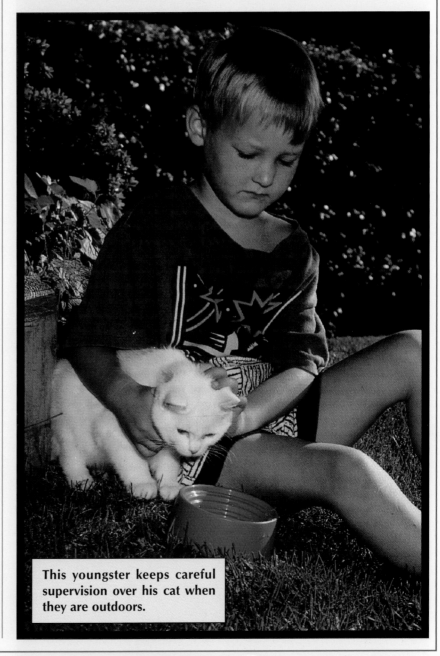

This youngster keeps careful supervision over his cat when they are outdoors.

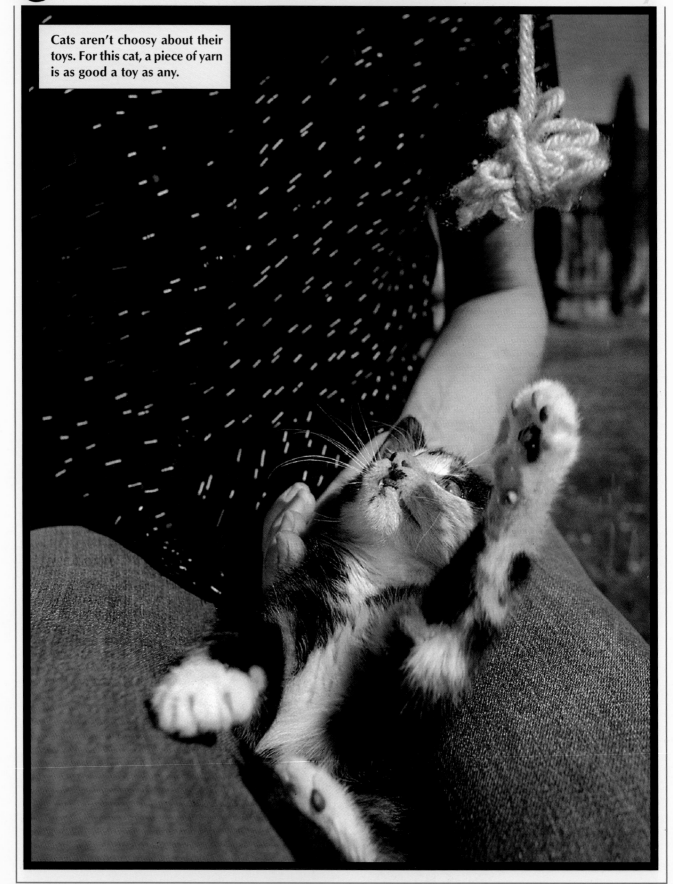

Cats aren't choosy about their toys. For this cat, a piece of yarn is as good a toy as any.

CHOOSING A KITTEN OR CAT

Having decided that you are definitely going to obtain a kitten or a cat, there are a number of considerations that the genuine cat lover will need to carefully ponder so that the right choice is made.

KITTEN OR CAT?

For most, but not all, potential owners, a kitten will be the preferred choice. They are really amusing—the more so if you obtain two at the same time. They will provide company for each other while you are out at work. The drawback is that kittens will require a lot more attention than will an adult, and they are more mischievous as well. The adult cat will already be more set in its ways and may be the sort that will wander off.

It will be much harder to introduce an adult cat into a household that has a dog, but it is possible, depending on the nature of the dog more than the cat. Even so, many people, this author's family included, have taken in adults as well as kittens and been very pleased with them. More elderly people may find the adult a better choice. If you are interested in exhibiting or breeding cats, these aspects would influence your choice. In either case, I would suggest the young adult might be the wisest option. This is because the older kitten/young adult will be more mature, thus its quality will be more readily ascertained. However, such a cat will be rather more expensive. This fact might mean that you have to take a little more risk and go for a younger animal.

AGE TO PURCHASE

If you have never owned a cat before, then it would be wise to obtain a kitten that is about 10-16 weeks of age. Such a kitten will be more established. In all probability, it will have been vaccinated against the major feline diseases. It is quite possible to rear a kitten from six weeks of age, but this will require your

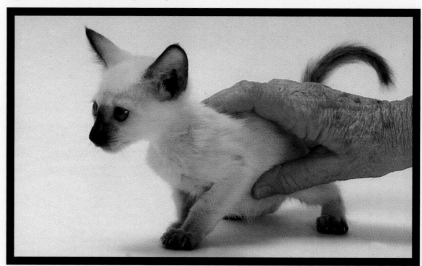

Nine-week-old chocolate point Siamese kitten.

devoting much more time to it. Generally, such a path is not recommended for the first-time cat owner. With a young adult required for exhibition or breeding, a sound age would be when it is about nine or more months of age.

PUREBRED OR MOGGIE?

Unlike dogs, in which mongrels can grow to be any size and may look like a really mixed bag, the moggie (mixed breed) cat often looks more beautiful than many pure-breds. Their size will not be a factor that you need to ponder because all cats are within a tolerable range. If you plan to breed cats, or to seriously exhibit, a purebred has to be the only choice. Even if you want a cat only as a companion, you may have a particular liking for one of the pure-bred varieties, and in a particular color.

Bear in mind that cats are currently extremely popular pets and a thriving market has developed for stolen purebred cats, especially kittens. If you are not concerned about the ancestry of your pet, the moggie is possibly the best choice. Or, perhaps you could have one of each type?

COAT TYPE

I would say without hesitation that for the first-time owner, a short- or medium-haired kitten or cat would be the best choice.

Only if you know that you have the time and inclination to devote fifteen or so minutes each day to grooming should you consider the longhaired breeds, such as Persians. Shorthaired breeds need only infrequent brushing because they keep their coats looking immaculate. Persian types will quickly become a mass of tangles if they are not groomed daily. You can always obtain a longhaired breed once you are sure that you are a really dedicated cat lover.

I would also add that for the novice owner, he should restrict his choice to breeds that show no alteration to the basic anatomy of the cat. On this account, breeds with no tail, no hair, or any other genetic alteration to their structure, are best left until experience has been gained with cats. This still leaves you with a considerable range of cats from which to choose—and in all of the colors and patterns known to exist in cats.

MALE OR FEMALE?

If you are having the kitten or cat as a companion only, then it does not matter which sex it is: both sexes are loving and affectionate. If you plan to breed, the queen should be your first choice. Owning a whole (unneutered) tom cat presents many problems. He will be marking his territory

A longhaired Scottish Fold sporting beautiful pelage. This breed, which also comes in a shorthaired version, is characterized by its folded ears, which are the result of a mutation.

(your home) with his scent—a rather unpleasant pungent sort of aroma that I would rank only just a little better than that of a skunk! The latter at least disappears quite quickly, whereas that of the tom is being constantly added to.

The whole tom will be out and about maintaining his outdoor territory and will be fighting any would-be intruder more willingly than will the neutered tom. Further, if you are to become a breeder, you will ideally use the services of a leading stud of proven ability at siring litters, and stamping his type on them.

If the kitten or cat is to be solely a pet, then please see that it is neutered. The small cost involved is worth every penny paid. You will not be hit with a succession of litters.

In the case of the tom, it will not be marking its territory all of the time, nor landing someone else with unwanted kittens that end up in the local animal shelter, or worse, being abandoned. It makes you wonder about people when cats are disposed of in these ways. You can reduce the incidence of this happening by neutering or spaying your pet.

HOW TO CHOOSE A KITTEN OR CAT

In selecting a suitable kitten or cat, there are two aspects that are likely to be important. In the case of the potential breeder/exhibitor, he will want a quality kitten. The reality is that you cannot be advised of such selection from a book. You must do

> **When selecting a kitten, it does not matter which sex it is. Either sex can make a loving and affectionate pet.**

some background research and locate a breeder of reputation. This done, you can do no more than place your trust in such a person to guide you in your selection. In most instances, you will get what you pay for: so don't expect to get a show stopper at a pet price—it never happens.

Another consideration is in regard to the health of the kitten, or cat, irrespective of its quality. You will appreciate that the purchase of any living creature, especially a young one, carries with it a degree of risk, so it is a case of reducing this to its most

acceptable level. There is no one source that is guaranteed to sell you a cat that will survive, but some sources are more risky than others. First, however, we will look at key points to note when you inspect kittens and cats.

1. Begin by watching which kittens seem the most outgoing. These are your best choice. The timid kitten that is afraid to approach you is likely to turn out very nervous—it may also be more prone to illness.
2. Notice the kittens at play and watch for those that show signs of a disability in their movements. They may only be suffering from a rough-and-tumble strain, or they may have an impediment to their

limbs. Rule out any that display a problem.

3. Now you can make a physical examination of the kitten. Begin with the head.

The *eyes* should be round and bright with no signs of weeping. A cat has what is called a haw, or third eyelid. It is the nictitating membrane and is seen in the lower corner of the eye. If it is raised over part of the eye, this invariably indicates a problem—slight though this may be. However, it could be serious, so if seen this would mean a rejection. The *nose* should be dry with no signs of congealed mucus. Open the kitten's *mouth* and smell its breath. The odor should not be unpleasant. The *teeth* will be small and white with no build up of tartar on them in a kitten. They should be either a level bite (the incisors of the upper jaw just touching those of the lower jaw), or they will be a scissor, or pincer, bite (the upper incisors just overlapping the lower ones). An undershot jaw (lower incisors protruding in front of those of the upper jaw) is undesirable but is seen in some breeds. The *ears* will be erect, well furred, and with no visible abrasions. They should be sweet smelling. Brown wax in the ears is a sign of parasitic activity. It is not a major problem if it is promptly attended to, but it is not a good sign. The *fur* of a kitten will not be quite as profuse as in the adult, but it will look healthy. It should smell pleasant. Part the fur to inspect for parasites. Small blackish-red specks indicate flea dirt, so look further— behind the ears and at the base of the tail. Fleas are very mobile, whereas lice are gray and slow moving. They indicate poor living conditions. Any bald areas indicate a problem, especially if they are in the form of whorls, which are the result of fungal attack. The *abdomen* should be well filled without being pot bellied, which might suggest worm infestation. It should be free of abrasions. *Feet*: There

> **The considerably long life span of cats—around 15 to 20 years or so—means that you can have a goodly number of years to enjoy your feline friend.**

should be five toes on the front feet and four toes on the hind feet. Each toe should have a claw. The pads on the paws should be soft in a kitten but harder in an adult. Sometimes a cat may have six toes, termed polydactyly. This is not a problem in a pet cat but is a no-no in an exhibition or breeding animal. Declawed cats are ineligible for exhibition under nearly all registration body rules. The *tail* should ideally be kink free in an exhibition or breeding cat. Kinks are more likely to be found in foreign breeds.

You may not have the opportunity of seeing the fecal matter of a kitten or cat, but if you do, it should be firm and not liquid. Any blood streaks in it are a clear sign of an

Top: Red classic tabby and white longhaired American Curls. Bottom: Selkirk Rex kittens. A healthy kitten will be bright eyed, alert, and in full coat. When selecting a kitten, health should be your primary consideration.

internal disorder. It should be added that the bowel movements of kittens are much more changeable than those of the adult. This being so, a change in diet, a slight cold, in fact many causes can result in the feces of a kitten becoming rather more liquid, but they should never be like water.

If you are selecting an adult cat, you must make sure it can be handled. Take due caution when lifting it up; an adult can inflict serious damage to your face with its claws. Some cats that are otherwise quite friendly do not take kindly to strangers suddenly lifting them up. If the cat is clearly of an aggressive nature, do not select it regardless of how attractive it is—this applies doubly so if you have children in your home.

WHERE TO OBTAIN A KITTEN OR CAT

The answer to this question will be dependent on why the cat is being purchased. For a quality exhibition or breeding feline, you must obviously seek out a suitable breeder — preferably in your locality, so that you can become friends with them. You may wish to

> **Persian. If you have your heart set on this very popular breed of cat, remember that you will have to regularly devote time to a grooming regimen.**

acquire more of their stock as you become established. Do not purchase a show cat from a breeder solely because the breeder is local; such a person must have a good reputation. Make inquiries at local shows and via your vet. Time spent in research is rarely wasted: it could save you a great deal of future costs.

For the potential pet owner, naturally the pet shop is the first source that comes to mind. Be sure that a kitten sold in a store is already vaccinated against the major feline diseases and you should be just fine.

Finally, have your vet give the kitten a thorough physical checkup—regardless of the source.

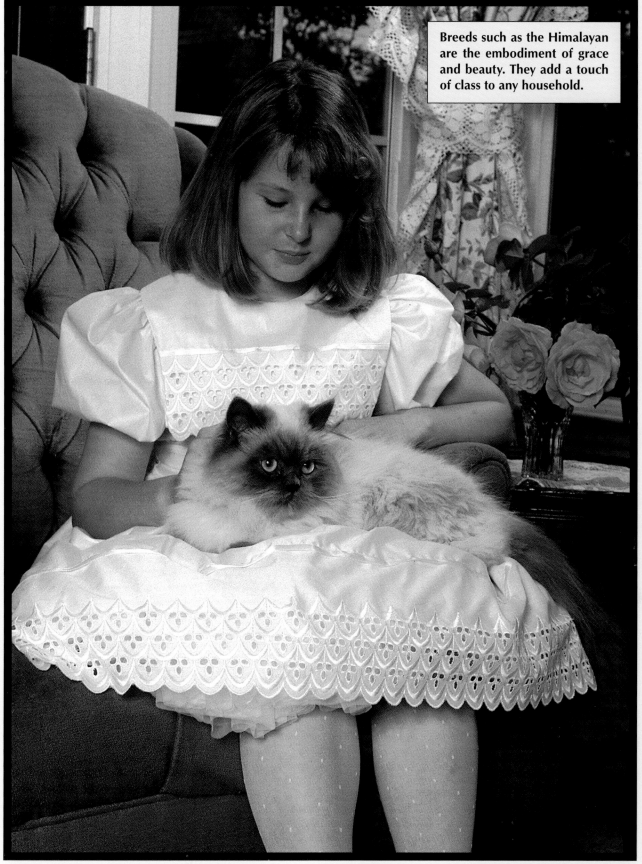

Breeds such as the Himalayan are the embodiment of grace and beauty. They add a touch of class to any household.

A Javanese queen meticulously grooming her youngster. In essence, Javanese are longhaired Colorpoint Shorthairs.

FEEDING

Feeding your cat or kitten is basically very simple, given the number of commercial cat foods now available. As long as you have a good can opener and a modicum of useful information, you are in business—it really is that easy. The essential information in regard to feline feeding is as follows:

1. The cat is a prime carnivore, so its diet must reflect this fact. It should contain a goodly percentage of protein in the form of meat, poultry, or fish.

2. All food given to cats should be fresh. Apart from the fact that well-cared-for cats will turn their nose up at most foods that are not fresh, there is the obvious danger to them of becoming ill from bacteria in stale or "off" food. If you don't like the look or smell of a food item, the simple rule is to trash it.

3. Try to give your kitten plenty of variety when it is young. This reduces (though does not eliminate) the likelihood of it becoming a faddy eater when it matures. Apart from this, the wider the variety the less likely it

will be that an important ingredient is missing. The reality of feeding cats is that if you feed them on the best brands of canned foods and dry kibble, they will refuse the cheaper brands. Most of us spoil our cats, so if they are brought up on quality brands, be sure you at

With the wide variety of commercial cat foods that are on the market today, there is no reason for your cat to have a boring diet. Your vet can suggest a feeding program that is right for your cat.

least vary these between the beef, poultry, and fish offerings. Be warned that too much fish food is not good for your kitty: many cats will return this shortly afterward—via vomiting!

4. Avoid feeding food that contains fine bones. Cats enjoy meat on the bone; it

is the splinter types that should be avoided.

5. If fresh meat is given, it must be of a standard fit for human consumption.

6. Do not try to trim the food bill by giving your cat the brands prepared for dogs. These contain a higher percentage of carbohydrates and not enough protein for a cat. This is why they are less expensive in the first place.

WHEN TO FEED AND HOW MUCH

Cats should be fed little and often, whenever this is convenient to your daily routine. The actual feeding times are not important at all, but they should be regular once times have been established. Some people feed twice a day, some three. In our household, we are at home all day so the cats are fed on an ad lib basis throughout the day. This means certain of them will get maybe three feeds, others as many as five to seven, depending on the cat in question. All cats differ in the amount they will eat: some are small eaters, while others are little piggies.

The amount to feed is linked to how often you are feeding and the quality of the food. If your cats get a number of meals, they will clearly eat smaller amounts than if they only have two or three meals a day. A high-protein content food will satiate the cat more readily than will a dish full of rice, bits of vegetable leftovers, and a few scraps of meat. The two basic guides as to whether or not you are feeding your cat well enough are:

1. Does it look well muscled and exhibit a gorgeous-looking sleek coat?
2. Does it walk away from its dish in a satisfied manner or is it licking up every last bit and clearly wanting more? In the latter instance, it probably is not getting enough. If it leaves some food on its plate at every meal, and if the quality of the food is good, then you can reduce the quantity. You will establish the right amount on a trial and error basis.

FEEDING KITTENS

There are special brands of kitten food available if you want them. When feeding dry cat food, you must be sure the pieces are small enough for the kitten to crunch. Kittens have small and rather weak teeth, so they cannot cope with kibbled food too well until they are about ten or more weeks of age. You can provide dried cat food on an ad lib basis, so the kitten and adults can have it whenever they wish. You will find that some cats prefer dried food while others partake of a few kibbles only every so often.

Water should always be available to your kitten and cats, even if they drink very little of it. This is more likely if

their basic diet is of moist canned food, which contains a high percentage of water. A young kitten should receive four or more meals per day.

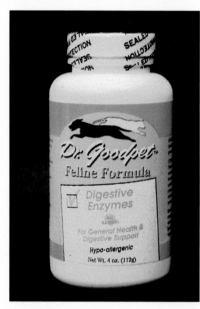

Older cats particularly can suffer from problems caused by a slowing or failing digestive system. Fortunately, these can be alleviated with attention to diet. Photo courtesy of Dr. Goodpet; call (800)222-9932 for the pet dealer near you.

COMMERCIAL FOOD

Apart from food specially packaged or canned for cats, there are many kitchen items that your kitten or cat will enjoy. These should be chopped up into pieces that are small enough for your pet to cope with.

Fresh meat: Cut up a few pieces from the meat you are having. For kittens, it must be scraped or minced into very small pieces. Liver is rich in vitamins, but much is lost during cooking. Do not supply too much liver; otherwise, the kitten or cat will have a stomach upset.

Fish: These are rich in proteins and essential amino acids. They are best steamed or grilled. Sardines and other fish canned in oils will be greatly enjoyed periodically and are rich in vitamins. Do not overfeed canned fish as it will prove too rich for young kittens.

Eggs: This food is rich in protein. Serve boiled and chopped.

Cheese: This is rich in protein and greatly enjoyed in small amounts by most cats. It can be served as is or cooked with other food.

Carbohydrates: Examples are bread, pasta, rice, and unsweetened breakfast cereals. Some cats will tolerate a small amount of carbohydrates mixed with meat;

Treats can be provided on an occasional basis to help provide a little variety in the diet. Some treats act as a cleansing agent to help reduce tartar on the cat's teeth. Photo courtesy of Heinz.

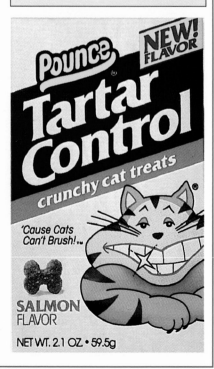

others will all but ignore such food. This will depend on how well fed they are. Carbohydrates are not essential food items for cats but are included in commercial diets to provide bulk and to keep the cost down. They are the cheapest and most readily available source of energy food, but are of no value in terms of building muscle tissue.

Fruit and vegetables: In the wild, these are supplied via the stomach contents of the cat's prey. In such, they are partially digested and thus can be assimilated in the cat's body. A cat cannot utilize raw vegetable matter, so it must be boiled first so that the tough cellulose walls are broken down. Small amounts of vegetables and fruits can be mixed in with freshly cooked meats.

Sweet Items: Cats do not have a sweet tooth as do dogs so are rarely interested in items such as cakes or sweet cookies. This is just as well as these items are not good for their teeth.

Right: In addition to their food, cats should have access to fresh water at all times. Do not give your cat milk, as it can cause digestive problems. Bottom: Dry kibbled food can be provided on an ad lib basis; canned food should not be left out for any great length of time because it can spoil.

GENERAL CARE

Cats are no problem at all to cater to in their day-to-day management, but when a kitten is arriving into your home, you should be aware of potential dangers. Adult cats are very cautious creatures, but kittens are adventurous and learn about dangers only as they mature. You must therefore think for them.

1. Do not leave irons and other electrical appliances plugged into sockets. A kitten may try to climb the cords or bite into them.

2. Be sure that any balconies are screened so that the kitten is in no danger of falling off.

3. Be sure that washing and drying machine doors are always closed because kittens have been known to clamber in and then decide to take a nap! Fish tanks should be fitted with canopies so that the kitten is in no danger of falling into them. Open fireplaces must be protected with a suitable mesh guard.

6. Houseplants should be well out of reach of the kitten, as some are poisonous.

7. Trash cans should be secured so that the kitten cannot rummage through them. They may contain dangerous items, such as

the sharp edges of food cans, which the kitten might lick.

8. Young children should never be left alone with kittens. They do not understand how delicate these are. This also applies to a dog if you

Your feline friend will reap the benefits of proper nutrition: healthy skin and coat, bright eyes, plenty of energy, and all-around good health. Photo courtesy of Nutro. Call (800)833-5330 for the pet dealer nearest you.

have one. They are only safe together once they are well acquainted.

9. Cherished items, such as ornaments, are best placed well out of reach of a kitten, which might easily knock them from low shelves it might clamber onto.

A KITTEN'S FIRST DAYS IN YOUR HOME

When it is time to pick up your kitten, try to do this early in the day so the kitten has plenty of time to settle into its new home.

Be sure to ask the seller what feeding regimen the kitten is familiar with. Stick to this for a week, and then gradually make any desired changes. This will remove the risk of an upset stomach due to the sudden upheaval in the kitten's life. You will also need the kitten's vaccination certificates, and its pedigree and registration transfer forms if these are applicable.

If the journey home is a long one, take the carry box, or a cut-down cardboard box, lined with toweling for the kitten to sleep on. It may be sick so be prepared for this. Have water and maybe some dry cat food with you, and make periodic stops so its stomach has a few minutes rest from the vehicle's momentum, which it will not be used to. It would be wise to also take a litter tray, complete with some litter, on long journeys. Once back at home, you can start by letting the kitten explore the kitchen. It might appreciate some water and may even be hungry. It may also wish to have a sleep. Do not let children pester it. It will urinate very soon after it has drank, been to sleep, or been playing, and will want to defecate shortly after eating. Its litter tray should be placed in a convenient location.

If the kitten has not been vaccinated, or if the vaccinations are not yet effective (about four weeks from date given), do not let the kitten out of doors. When it is bedtime, place the kitten in its carry box, bed, or wherever it is to sleep. By all means supply a cuddly toy if you have only the one kitten, and this will in some way offset the fact that it no longer has its littermates to curl up next to. You may decide to let it sleep on your bed, but if this is to be done you should not change your mind as the kitten grows up.

LITTER TRAINING

A kitten cannot control its bowels for very long so you must be watchful at certain times as already mentioned. The kitten will begin to cry and will start to look around for a secluded spot in which to attend its toiletry needs. When you see it doing this, you must act promptly and place the kitten in its litter tray.

Gently hold its paws and scratch them into the litter. It will usually oblige. If not, and it jumps out of the tray, you must continue to watch it and repeat the operation. It will very quickly catch on as to what is required. You must, however, accept that the odd accident will happen. The tray must be kept clean; otherwise, the kitten will not be encouraged to use it.

SCRATCHING POST TRAINING

This is done in much the same manner as litter training. When you see the kitten start to claw at the carpet or the furniture, quickly lift it up and take it to the scratching post. You can draw its paws down the post and, once again, after a few lessons it will understand it is allowed to scratch this, but not the

It's important to keep your cat's litter box clean, and a variety of litters is available to make your job easier. Photo courtesy of Swheat Scoop/Pet Care Systems, Inc. Call (800)SWEATS for the pet dealer nearest you.

furniture. As it gets older you can say "no" in a firm voice if it goes to scratch anything. You can also give it a light tap on its hindquarters—providing you can actually catch it in the act. Such discipline will be meaningless if it is given even a few seconds after the kitten has committed a misdemeanor. Always remember that cats, like dogs, relate only to the present, not to the past.

LEAD TRAINING

Cats are not happy on a lead even though some will tolerate one if trained from a young age. They feel very exposed and vulnerable when constrained. If they are startled by something, they will immediately struggle to free themselves, and will then panic and run off. If they are in a strange environment, you may lose your pet. I would therefore not recommend the average pet owner to attempt lead training their cat. Cats of foreign type usually respond better to lead training than do other breeds. If you do decide to train your cat to walk on a lead, never attempt to drag it. Let it go where it wants, then slowly, once it is familiar with the restraint of a lead, you can gently persuade it to travel in the direction that you wish. Fit the cat with a harness so that you have more control over it should it suddenly panic.

GROOMING

Grooming a shorthaired cat is simplicity itself. However, it should be done on a regular basis, both in order that the cat becomes used to being handled, and so you can take the opportunity to give it a physical check. Use the brush to groom with the lie of the hair, commencing on its neck. When the brushing is completed, you can then use the fine comb and repeat the operation. Take care when combing its underbelly as this is more sensitive. Finish with a silk or chamois leather to give the coat a nice shine.

Examine the cat's ears, teeth, and fur for any signs of parasites. Longhaired cats need grooming daily. Commence with a brisk brushing with the lie of the fur, then brush against it, and finally back with the lie. This should remove tangles and most debris that may be clinging to it. Next you can use the wide- or medium-toothed comb to groom with the lie—then against it. Should you feel any stiff resistance, find the offending tangle and tease it out with your fingers. At all times you must be as gentle as possible; otherwise, the cat will soon come to dislike being groomed. You can end by using the fine-toothed comb, and by using a stiff toothbrush on the fur of the face.

If the cat should get dirty, which is unusual for cats, you can clean it by sprinkling talcum powder or powdered chalk into the fur, then thoroughly groom it out. Be sure it is well groomed out as longhaired cats always spend much time licking their fur. If you decide the cat needs a bath, be very sure that longhaired cats are extremely well groomed prior to the bath; otherwise the fur will become badly matted, and you will find it very difficult to groom out the tangles. When bathing, take great care that no water enters its eyes, as this will make a difficult task even more so. It will usually be helpful if someone assists you with the bathing—one to hold the cat and one to attend to the actual washing.

The shampoo must be thoroughly rinsed out of the fur; otherwise, it will make it sticky and could cause an irritation. Be sure the water is only lukewarm, and ensure that the cat is not allowed out of doors until it is thoroughly dry.

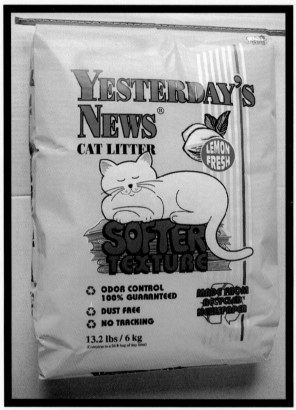

Cat litter has come a long way since the days of dried clay! Today's litters are dust-free, super-absorbent and don't get stuck in kitty's paws. Photo courtesy of Yesterday's News®.

HANDLING KITTENS AND CATS

Never lift a kitten or cat up by the scruff of its neck: this is quite incorrect. It should always be supported under its chest with one hand while being secured to your chest with the other.

Children must be taught to handle a kitten with great

respect because, from an early age, even a kitten can inflict a very nasty scratch to a child's face or arms if it is handled in other than a gentle manner. Some cats will allow you to cradle them baby fashion on their backs; others will resent this and struggle to get free. Never insist that the pet cat be held in an unnatural position. The show cat must be handled very often from a young age so that it shows no resentment of this—or by being raised at arms length by a stranger: this is how the judge will inspect the exhibit.

If you find that your cat does become aggressive when being handled, and if you must place it into its carry box in order to transport it to the vet or elsewhere, be sure you have a good hold of its two front legs—behind the elbow. Next, secure a firm hold of the rear legs; otherwise, these will quickly rake your arm.

Alternatively, place a towel over the cat's body, which will reduce its ability to scratch you. If you have handled a cat from the time it was a kitten, you should not have problems; but adopted adults may be a different matter, even though they are otherwise friendly. They may not like being placed into a carry box, for example.

TRAVELING WITH CATS

Like people and dogs, some cats travel well in cars; others never take to it. Even good traveling cats may initially

Now what do I do?!!!

start to howl, or be sick, but thereafter they settle down without further problem. Never allow the cat to be loose in a car if you are the sole occupant. Do not give travel sickness pills without your vet's advice. The vet may be able to supply a better sedative if this is needed. Never leave your cat in a vehicle on hot days. The cat could die from heat exhaustion. If a cat is clearly suffering from heat stroke, you must bring its body temperature down as rapidly as possible. Soak it in a wet towel, or dunk it into a tub of cool water (but not its head, which can be wiped with a cold piece of cloth).

TRAVELING ABROAD

When a cat is transported by air or sea, it must be placed into a secure container, such as a carry box. Airlines and shippers may differ in the exact requirements of a container, so you are advised to check this out well in advance of any such journey.

You should also check with the country of destination what regulations they may have in regard to importing cats into their country. For example, all livestock entering Great Britain, Australia, New Zealand, Hawaii, and certain other countries, must go through a six-month quarantine period. Cats are not required at this time to go into quarantine when entering the US, but must have satisfactory veterinary health certificates. The same is generally true when entering mainland European countries, which may additionally require proof of vaccination against rabies. Regulations can change at any time, so reference to old

literature may be out of date. Your veterinarian will be able to help you in finding out the current regulations.

VACATIONS

In general, cats do not enjoy accompanying you on vacation. They are territorial creatures, and so would rather remain in the familiar environment of their own home. This so, when you go away try to arrange for a relative or friend to call in each day and feed your cat, and maybe spend a few minutes with it. This is preferable to placing it in a cattery that boards felines. If you do board your cat, inspect the boarding establishment first so that you are satisfied that they have a competent staff and adequate accommodations. A veterinary recommendation is preferred. Any worthwhile cattery will insist on seeing current certificates of vaccination against the major feline diseases.

INTRODUCING CATS TO OTHER PETS

If you already have a cat, a dog, or a large parrot, the introduction of a kitten or cat may go smoothly, or may present problems, depending on the temperament of the resident pets and the newcomer. Kittens are generally less difficult to introduce because they are not aware that they may not be appreciated by the other pets. They simply want to make friends. An adopted adult cat, on the other hand, may have had a bad experience with other animals, so it may be less charitable about making friends. Other cats will be curious about the newcomer,

who will approach them with caution. They will probably sniff the kitten, hiss at it, and move away. They may even box its ears a few times. However, they are aware that it is a baby of their own kind so will normally just ignore it initially. As the days go by, they will get used to it. Some adults will become a sort of aunt or uncle to the kitten and will soon be playing with it. Others will eventually accept it without ever getting on really friendly terms.

When an adult cat is introduced to a home with a resident feline, the newcomer may be accepted without problem, or the fur may start to fly. There is nothing you can do to make cats be friendly with each other or other pets. They must sort their relationships out between themselves.

If a dog is the other pet, only you know its nature. You must beware that it does not attack the kitten. Even if it is known to chase cats, it may well accept the kitten—given time. Some will play happily with cats; others treat them with quiet indifference. Never hold a kitten in front of another pet, as this is courting disaster.

Large parrots usually ignore kittens after they have had time to study them. Most kittens, and indeed cats, will not wish to press their attentions on any large parrot that is equipped with a raucous voice and a powerful beak. It should go without saying, until you are very sure of how the kitten or cat is being accepted by other non-cat residents, you should never leave them alone together when you are not present.

cats quarterly

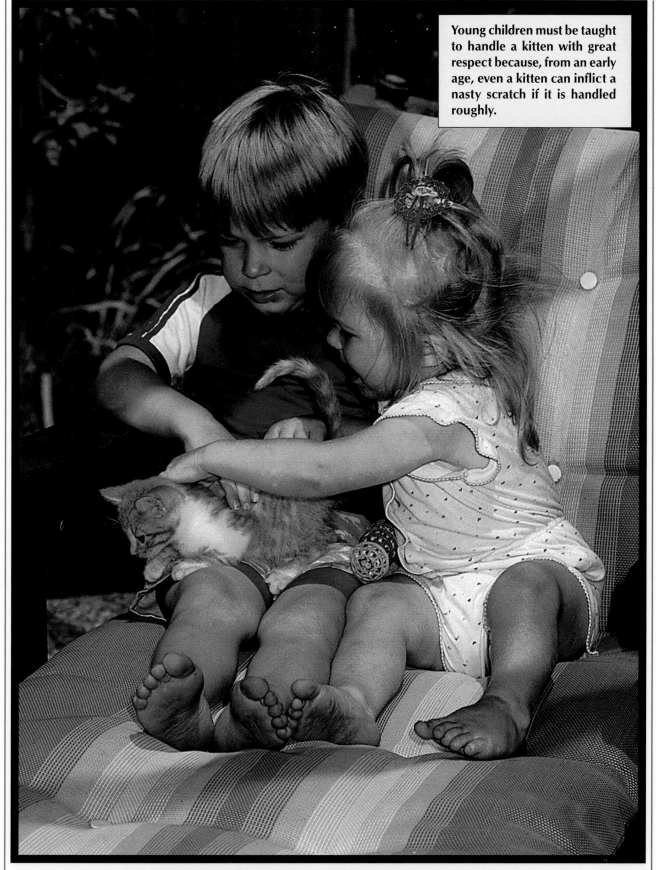

Young children must be taught to handle a kitten with great respect because, from an early age, even a kitten can inflict a nasty scratch if it is handled roughly.

HEALTH

Although you might think that disease has little merit, it is in fact a vital part of survival. It ensures that only the fittest live to perpetuate their species. It is a regulator that thins down excessive numbers in the wild habitat. It is thus an essential part of the complex web of life. This said, none of us want to see our cherished pets die, or even suffer, because of an illness.

The ways that we can prevent this from happening are threefold:

1. By ensuring that our cats are well fed and well managed.
2. By recognizing the signs of ill health.
3. By ensuring that we take prompt action to arrest disease or ill health should they occur.

The first course of action has been covered in earlier chapters, so here we can review numbers 2 and 3.

RECOGNIZING ILL HEALTH

A cat cannot tell us when it feels ill, so the only way we can know is by observation. This will reveal an illness in one of two ways. Either the cat will display clinical signs of a problem, or its behavior will not be normal. To appreciate the latter, we must be aware of what normality is for the cat in question. The greedy eater may suddenly show lack of interest in its food. The energetic cat will be less so. All ill cats will tend to seek quiet spots where they can lay down and sleep.

Clinical signs of ill health are any or all of the following:

1. A discharge from the eyes or nose.
2. Dull eyes, with the haw becoming very visible.
3. Dull and staring coat. A very dry coat.
4. A cat that constantly coughs or makes a wheezing sound when breathing. All cats cough now and again, but this is different from the continual coughing of the ill cat.

For premium health, you can find life-cycle care products and nutritional supplements for your kitten or cat that are 100% human-consumption grade so you're guaranteed quality and freshness. Photo courtesy of Noah's Kingdom. Call 800-662-4711 for the location of the dealer nearest you.

5. Vomiting. Cats will often vomit after eating grass (which acts as a natural purgative), eating a food that is too rich for their stomach, or simply because they have eaten too much (greedy feeders). This is totally different from the cat that is repeatedly sick, especially a few times during any 24-hour period.
6. If the cat scratches a great deal, this too would indicate a problem—such as parasites. Yet again, it must be appreciated that all cats like a good scratch every so often.
7. The bowel movements of a cat are normally reasonably firm in texture, so if they become loose, this would suggest a minor tummy upset or the first signs of something more serious. If they became more liquid, and maybe streaked with blood, this would definitely be abnormal.
8. If a cat suddenly starts to lose weight, something is amiss.
9. If a cat suddenly starts to drink a lot of water, yet its diet has not changed, then there is a problem

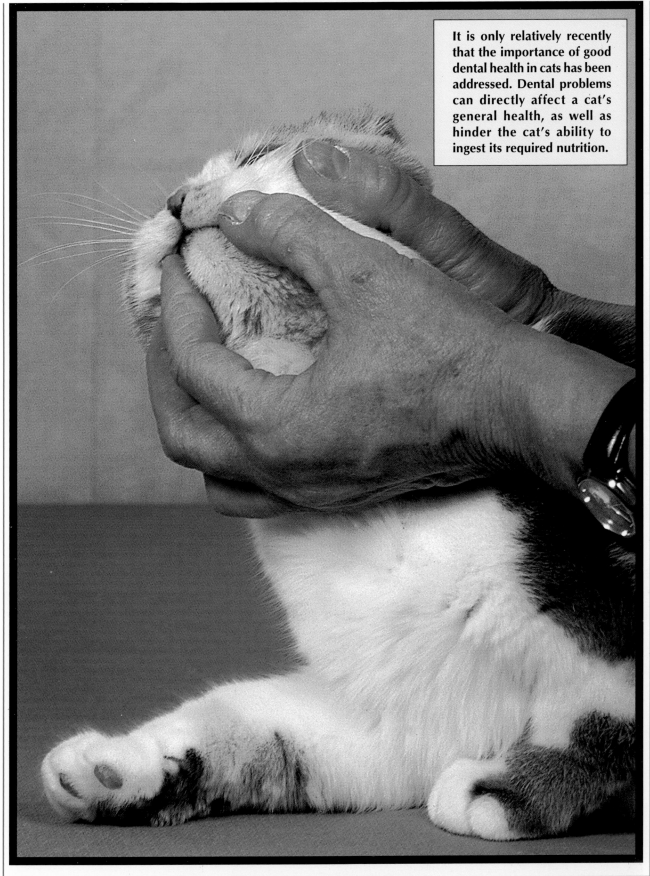

It is only relatively recently that the importance of good dental health in cats has been addressed. Dental problems can directly affect a cat's general health, as well as hinder the cat's ability to ingest its required nutrition.

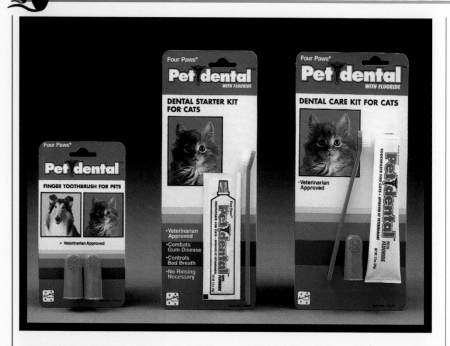

(assuming it is not just a case of the weather being unusually hot).

10. Bleeding. Any cat that bleeds from the mouth, the anus, the vulva, or the penis clearly has something wrong with it.

11. Impediment to its movement, or any other obvious anatomical problem.

There are a considerable number of diseases that a cat can suffer from, but only a limited number of ways that such problems can show themselves. This means that many of the clinical signs can cover a number of diseases. There is no way that an unqualified person can diagnose the problem —thus the treatment. This means that you must consult a veterinarian for all but the most minor of problems, and even they are not without risk. The problem may indeed be of a minor nature, but it may also be the beginning of a serious disease. How are you to tell? If you are wrong, the disease has had more time to become advanced, and it already had a head start before you noticed clinical signs.

If two or more of the signs noted above are being displayed by the cat, you need to consult your vet right away. If bleeding of any kind (other than from a minor cut) occurs, you must again consult your vet. If a supposedly minor condition does not improve within 24-48 hours, it is not minor.

TAKING PROMPT ACTION

For the vast majority of conditions, you should promptly call your vet. You should have first written down the clinical signs so that you do not forget anything. The vet will probably ask you about the cat's diet, state of its bowel movements, when it was last ill, if its vaccinations are up to date, and if anything in the cat's environment has changed recently. Based on this discussion, the vet will then suggest a course of action, which would normally be to visit the clinic so that he can give the cat a complete physical examination.

If the cat is suffering from parasitic infestation, such as lice or fleas, you must eradicate these quickly by using one of the modern remedies from your pet shop or veterinarian. They are usually effective against most common parasites. Fleas and mites leave the host for periods of time in order to lay eggs—lice spend their life cycle on the host. It is thus important that the bedding of a cat is thoroughly treated; otherwise, reinfestation will occur after treating the cat. It is best to burn blanketing after severe attacks.

Cuts: Minor cuts should be wiped clean with a mild antiseptic solution. Antiseptic ointment can be smeared onto the wound, but usually the cat will lick it off. For more serious cuts, the flow of blood should be stemmed by applying a lint and bandage, after first cleaning the wound. Be sure bandages are not too tight. Rush the cat to the vet.

Burns: These are of two kinds: chemical and direct heat. If the former, wash the skin by using plenty of water. If the burn is from direct heat, cool the site with water or an ice pack, then apply a thin film of an antibiotic. In both instances, consult the vet, who may need to treat the cat for shock. In severe cases, take emergency action as described, then wrap the cat in a blanket and rush it to the nearest vet.

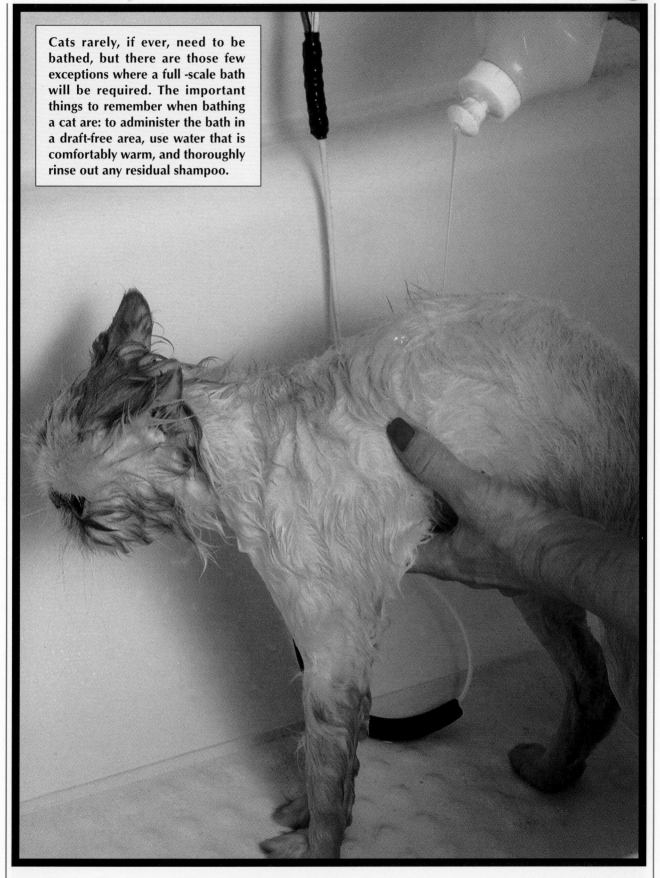

Cats rarely, if ever, need to be bathed, but there are those few exceptions where a full -scale bath will be required. The important things to remember when bathing a cat are: to administer the bath in a draft-free area, use water that is comfortably warm, and thoroughly rinse out any residual shampoo.

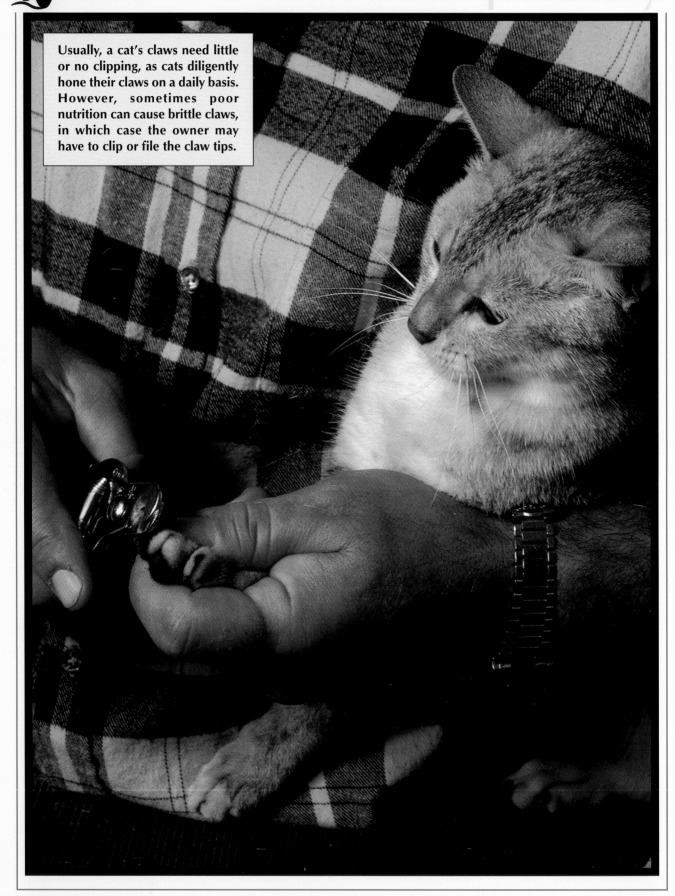

Usually, a cat's claws need little or no clipping, as cats diligently hone their claws on a daily basis. However, sometimes poor nutrition can cause brittle claws, in which case the owner may have to clip or file the claw tips.

Accidents: The course of action is to first move the cat to a safe place. Try to place a blanket or even a piece of cardboard under the cat so it can be moved. Avoid lifting its head to prevent blood from backing up into the throat and possibly blocking the air passages. Place a blanket over the cat to keep it warm, then either rush the cat to the vet or await his arrival, talking in a soothing manner to the cat. If shock is likely, place the cat in a darkened room if possible.

VACCINATIONS & MAJOR DISEASES

The respiratory and intestinal tracts, together with the heart, are three sources of major killer diseases in cats. You can protect the cat against some of them with vaccinations. You should contact your vet as soon as a kitten or cat is acquired if it has not already been vaccinated. Booster shots are required annually to ensure continued protection.

Feline influenza: This is caused by numerous viruses (microscopic bacteria). It is normally transferred by direct contact from one cat to another, or by the cat being in a place where an infected cat has been. High risk areas are catteries, cat shows, and veterinary clinics. Protection is via a vaccination given when the kitten is eight or more weeks of age. A booster is given about 21 days later, and the kitten is not fully protected until seven days after the booster.

Feline enteritis (Panleucopenia): This is

another viral disease, transmitted by direct/indirect contact or by a vector such as a flea. It is highly contagious but can be protected against by a vaccination given at the same time as that for cat flu.

Feline leukemia virus (FeLV): This dreaded disease

It only takes a minute for your cat or kitten to get lost—and yet it only takes a minute or so to get an I.D. tag that will protect your cat from being lost permanently. Protect your pet with the most visible identification system available: a tag. Photo courtesy of Quick Tag; for the location of the Quick Tag™ Engraving System machine nearest you, call 1-888-600-TAGS.

may show itself in a variety of ways, including anemia, vomiting, tumors, and acute diarrhea. Cats may become immune to it, but many die. It is highly contagious and spreads by direct contact with other cats. There is now a vaccination that helps protect cats against this disease. Your vet can test a cat for the virus. This is suggested when purchasing any costly feline. A certificate indicating that the kitten or cat is FeLV negative will then be supplied. It is advisable to insist on seeing a certificate when sending a queen to be mated.

VETERINARY TREATMENTS

When you are given tablets or liquids with which to dose your kitten or cat, it is essential that you follow the vet's instructions to the letter. Do not stop the treatment just because the cat appears to have made a dramatic recovery. This could result in a relapse and may also result in bacteria developing immunity against the medications given. Your vet will often supply vitamin pills when a treatment has been given. This is because medicines may not be selective in the bacteria they kill, meaning beneficial ones are also destroyed. These may include those responsible for the synthesis of certain vitamins, which will have been supplied orally pending the recolonization of the digestive tract with the needed organisms.

CAT BREEDS

The number of cat breeds that you can choose from will be between 35-50, depending on the country you live in and which cats are accepted as breeds by the differing registration authorities. However, the number of breeds in the UK is greatly in excess of 50 because, in the case of the Persian, for example, every color is regarded as a breed. In the US, the breed is Persian, and the colors are simply varieties of it. A brief discussion of the way domestic cats are classified will perhaps be both interesting and helpful to the newcomer to purebred cats, who is sometimes rather mystified by the apparent complexity of the subject.

DOMESTIC CAT CLASSIFICATION

The most basic division of the breeds is into groups based on coat length. There are thus longhairs and shorthairs. The longhairs comprise two quite distinct types. There are those of Persian origin, which have

> **European Shorthair. Some fanciers claim that this breed goes back to the days of the Roman Empire. This sturdy, medium-to-large breed is a very popular European house cat.**

profuse coats, and those of foreign origin. This latter term is used to describe the physical type. In essence, they have the conformation of a Siamese cat, whereas the Persian is a more stocky and solidly built feline. The shorthairs are likewise divisible into the European types, with cobby powerful bodies and round heads, and the foreigns. The latter, again, are most readily appreciated as being of the Siamese type—from which a number were developed. They have lithe bodies and a wedge-shaped head. Cats thus have three main basic ancestral stocks, with two subdivisions:

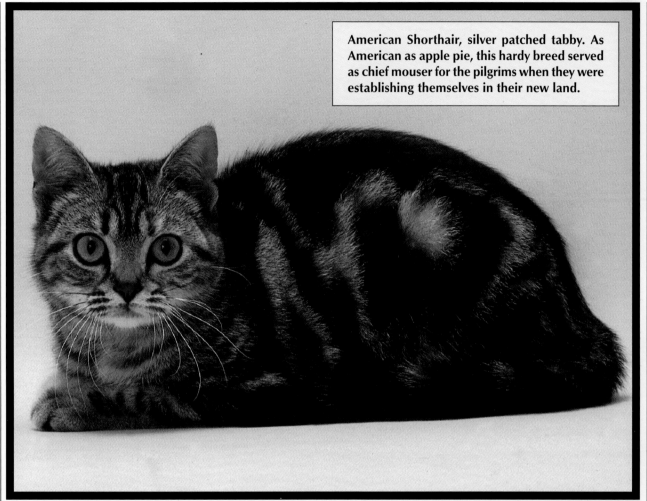

American Shorthair, silver patched tabby. As American as apple pie, this hardy breed served as chief mouser for the pilgrims when they were establishing themselves in their new land.

1. European Shorthairs of stocky type. The coat is thick, glossy, and short.
2. Persian cats. These have dense woolly fur, but originally there were two types: those with woolly fur and those with a much more silky texture. The latter are today exemplified by the Turkish breeds.
3. The foreigns. These are very slim, generally long-legged breeds. The Siamese is the best known example. Other foreigns are of Siamese type but more stocky and with rounder faces.

By interbreeding with these basic stocks, all present-day

Siamese queen and her kitten. Siamese cats are said to be the closest thing to a dog in a cat. They are known for their affectionate and attentive nature.

Top: Cymric. A longhaired version of the Manx, examples of this breed first appeared in Canada in the mid-1960s. The body is tailless and round, with a broad chest. The breed is available in a variety of colors and combinations of colors. **Bottom: Persian, red tabby.** This striking breed of cat is the most popular breed in the US. It is distinguished by its long, flowing coat and large, prominent eyes.

domestic cats have been produced. When a major mutation is transferred from one breed to another, or if it is an independent or new mutation, this will result in a new breed. For example, a longhaired Siamese is called a Balinese, while a longhaired Abyssinian is a Somali. When the Persian was crossed with the Siamese, the result became known as a Himalayan. This latter breed is now regarded as purely a color variant of the Persian in most US registrations. In Great Britain, the Himalayan of the US would be regarded as a Colourpoint Longhair. When the American Shorthair is crossed with the Burmese, the resulting cat is called a Bombay. New breeds are constantly in the making. In order to be accepted as such, they must fulfill certain criteria as laid down by the various cat registration associations. Some of the latter (for example, the Cat Fanciers' Association in the US, and the Governing Council of the Cat Fancy in Great Britain), are very particular about breed qualification. Others are less strict, which is why there are thus a variable number of recognized breeds. However, most of the long-established breeds are recognized by all registrations, including the famous Manx cat. This breed would not be accepted by a number of registrations were it not for its long establishment. It is based on a genetic abnormality that many associations today would outlaw.

Balinese. This breed is available in the same colors as in the Siamese. Balinese are slender, lithe cats with long plumy tails. In temperament, they are gentle and affectionate.

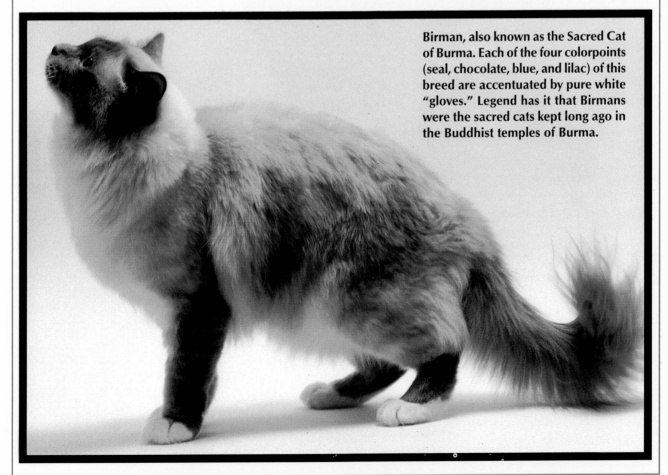

Birman, also known as the Sacred Cat of Burma. Each of the four colorpoints (seal, chocolate, blue, and lilac) of this breed are accentuated by pure white "gloves." Legend has it that Birmans were the sacred cats kept long ago in the Buddhist temples of Burma.

American Shorthair enjoying a meal. Its well-defined tabby pattern is seen in a number of other breeds.

COLORS AND PATTERNS

There are about twenty possible colors to be seen in cats, and they may have differing names in various countries. This can give the impression that there are substantially more colors than there actually are. From a genetic viewpoint, there are probably less than 16 colors, but they can range in shade as a result of breeder selection for lighter or darker tones. The same color may be given a different name from one country to another, so the chocolate of the UK is the champagne of the US. Further, a color term may be applied specifically to a given breed, so the sable of the Burmese would normally be called seal in most other breeds of Siamese origin. These differences, when crossing international borders, can make life difficult for the novice.

The patterns seen in cat coats are basically the following:

1. **Tabby patterns:** These may be mackerel (which is the wild type), blotched, or classic (which is the more popular type).
2. **Spots:** This pattern has gained considerably in popularity and is a feature of a number of the newer breeds now being established. It is not known for sure whether spotted patterns are independent patterns or the result of the break up of tabby stripes.
3. **Pointed (Siamese):** This pattern is known as Himalayan in most other pet animals. The extremities of the coat (face, ears, paws, and tail) are a darker shade than that of the body. This pattern is thermosensitive in that the points become paler as the temperature increases.
4. **Composites:** These are when two differing elements are combined. The bicolor, such as black and white, the tortoiseshell (and white), the cameos, and the blue-cream, are but a few of the vast number of potential composites.

Siamese, six-month-old seal point. The pointed pattern is thermosensitive: the points become paler as the temperature increases.

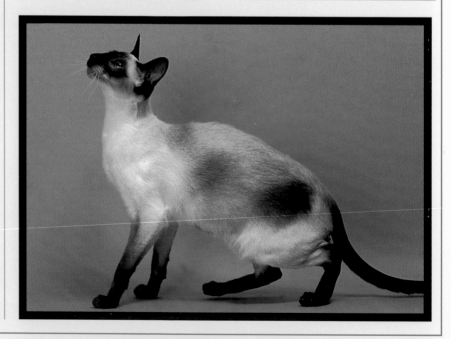

When the various colors are permuted with the coat patterns, the result is an incredible list of possibilities. In certain breeds, the color is a vital part of the breed. The Korat, for example, is a blue cat. In most breeds, however, the color is not so significant in determining breed status, therefore you can obtain the breed in whatever color varieties have been established at this time. In general, once a breed is established, it will be found that colors are then added to it.

When new colors are added, they may result in a new breed name being applied because in some breeds, such as the Siamese, the number of accepted colors is often limited by a given registration authority. Self-colored Siamese, for example, are known as Foreign Shorthairs in the UK, and Oriental Shorthairs in the US.

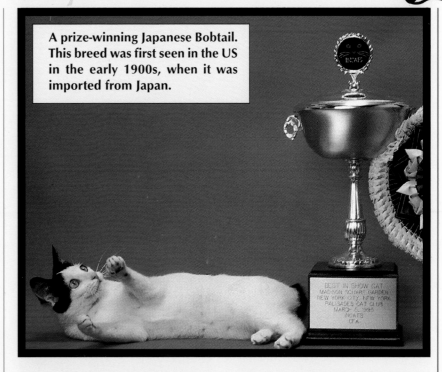

A prize-winning Japanese Bobtail. This breed was first seen in the US in the early 1900s, when it was imported from Japan.

A litter of Siamese kittens. It will be a while before the color of their face masks is fully developed.

In this book, all of the colors in a given breed will not be listed unless they are very limited in number. Once you decide on the breed of cat that you would like to own, and if you are really keen to know all about that breed, it is advisable to join the national breed club. You can also write to your chosen registration authority in order to obtain

the official standard of the breed, which will detail all colors available.

Not all breeds have full recognition, for they may be in the process of becoming established. This is an important point to remember if you plan to exhibit cats. The newer breeds may not have championship status, so they cannot compete for titles.

The following sections may enable you to note the breeds that are likely to be of particular interest to you in the selection process for your eventual pet.

LONGHAIRED BREEDS
Balinese: This is a longhaired Siamese resulting from a natural mutation in the Siamese, not from an introduced gene.

The coat is not excessive and gives the cat softer lines than the Siamese. In the US, the only colors permitted are seal, chocolate, blue, and lilac. Other colors are termed

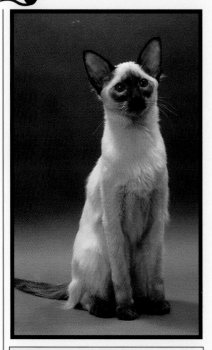

The Balinese is well muscled, lithe, and slender.

Javanese. In the UK, the latter would still be Balinese. This breed gained recognition during the 1970s.

Birman: Known as the "Sacred Cat of Burma." The coat is medium long, thus not too difficult to maintain. Breed features are the white paws and the darker points of the body. Colors are seal, blue, chocolate, and lilac, but others are possible. A very popular breed that arrived in Europe via France in 1919.

Lilac point Birman.

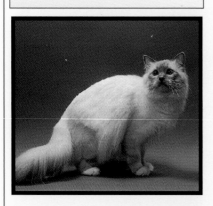

Established in the US during the late 1950s and in the UK during the 1960s.

Cymric: This is a longhaired Manx. The mutation appeared in North America during the 1960s. The coat is ample without being as woolly as in Persians. Not recognized in the UK.

Top: Cymric kitten. The Cymric is solidly constructed, with well-developed musculation. The coat is substantial but doesn't have the wool-like quality of the Persian. Below: Himalayan. This breed is also known as the Colourpoint Longhair or the Colorpoint Persian. In essence, it is a Persian with the markings of a Siamese.

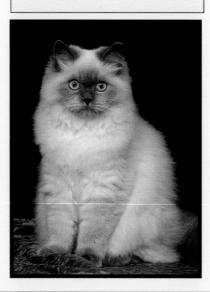

Himalayan: This is the result of crossing Persians with Siamese. It is thus a Persian with colorpoint markings. In the UK, it is called a Colourpoint Longhair. Most American registries now regard it as a color variation of the Persian, all traces of Siamese having been bred out many years ago.

Javanese: This is a Balinese in non-accepted colors in that breed. It may be any color that is recognized in Colorpoint Shorthairs. Not regarded as a separate breed in the UK, but just one of the numerous variants of a Balinese.

Lilac point Javanese. This breed comes in all of the colors that are permitted for the Colorpoint Shorthair.

Kashmir: Few associations regard this Persian as a separate breed. It is actually a self-colored Himalayan, usually lilac or chocolate. In the UK, it is a Colourpoint Longhair and in most US registries, it is a color variety of the Persian.

Maine Coon: This is the oldest breed of longhaired cat in the US. It was very popular in the early days of cat shows at the turn of the century. After losing devotees following the importation of

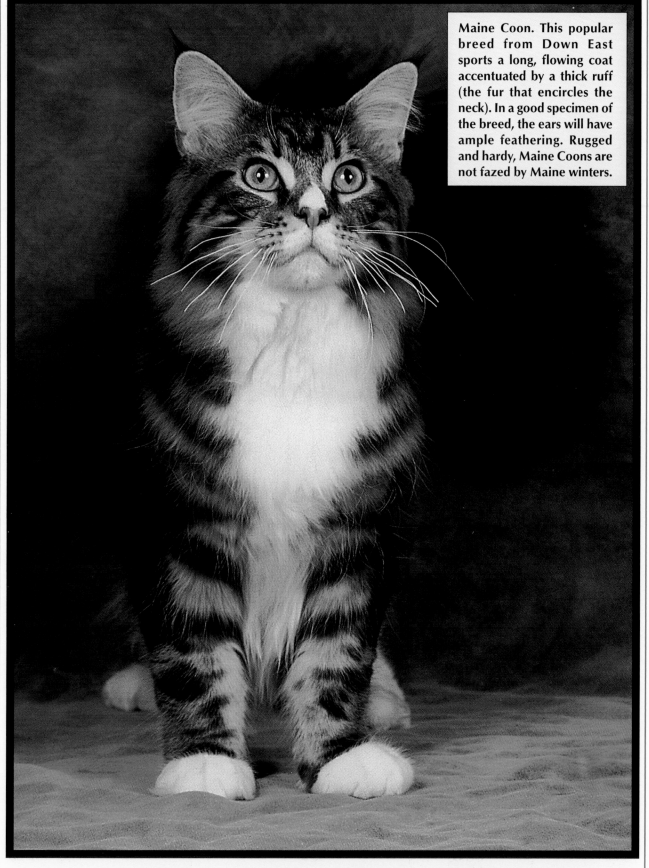

Maine Coon. This popular breed from Down East sports a long, flowing coat accentuated by a thick ruff (the fur that encircles the neck). In a good specimen of the breed, the ears will have ample feathering. Rugged and hardy, Maine Coons are not fazed by Maine winters.

exotic Eastern breeds, it has now made a comeback and its numbers are rising steadily. Its origin is thought to be the result of crosses between Turkish cats and the short-haired breeds that pertained at the time. It is a good-sized feline that is hardy and available in most colors other than the pointed.

Nebelung: This is a longhaired Russian Blue which has group V recognition with The International Cat Association (TICA) of the US. This means that any out-crosses can be used in order to try and establish this hybrid as a breed.

Norwegian Forest: Very similar in appearance to the Maine Coon, but it is an older breed. Like its American counterpart, it is a hardy breed that will shed its coat (but not its plume-like tail)

during the warmer summer months. Not commonly seen outside of its Norwegian homeland. Not a recognized breed in the UK.

Persian: This breed, numerically, is probably the most popular purebred cat seen in Western countries. It arrived into Europe from Persia during the 16th century. In the UK, it was known simply as a French cat for many years. Its coat has been selectively bred for in order to make it very profuse. Its facial shape has changed as well over the years and is now more rounded, as are the eyes. Persians come in just about every color and pattern known to exist in cats. They are docile and affectionate but do require daily grooming if their beautiful coat is to remain as such. In the UK, they are simply called

Persian. In addition to their beauty and grace, Persians are gentle, affectionate cats that relish the attention of their human family. It's no wonder why they are as popular as they are.

longhaired cats, each color and coat pattern being regarded as a breed. Many other breeds originated from crosses to Persians in order to introduce the longhaired gene.

Ragdoll: The basis of this breed is its docile and affectionate nature. It is a new breed with limited acceptance in the US; it is not recognized in the UK. Three color types are accepted: bicolor, colorpoint, and mitted. The fur is not excessive so is easily managed.

Ragdoll, frost bi-color. One of the newer breeds in the fancy, Ragdolls have coats that are virtually non-matting. Their sweet expression is enhanced by their big blue eyes.

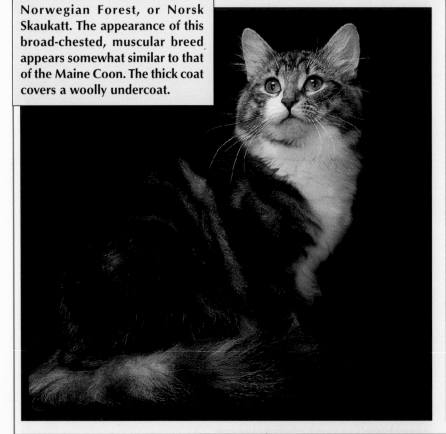

Norwegian Forest, or Norsk Skaukatt. The appearance of this broad-chested, muscular breed appears somewhat similar to that of the Maine Coon. The thick coat covers a woolly undercoat.

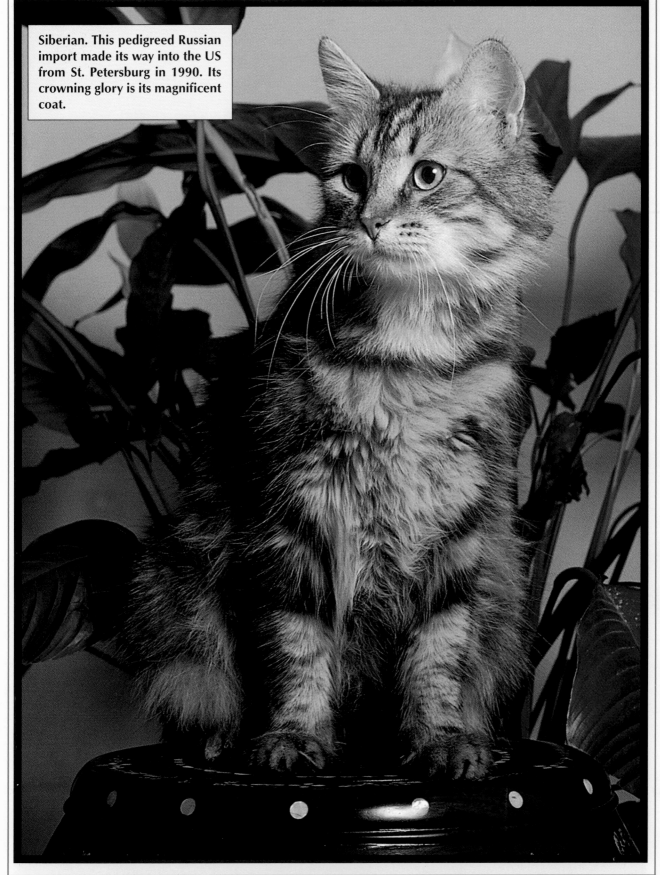

Siberian. This pedigreed Russian import made its way into the US from St. Petersburg in 1990. Its crowning glory is its magnificent coat.

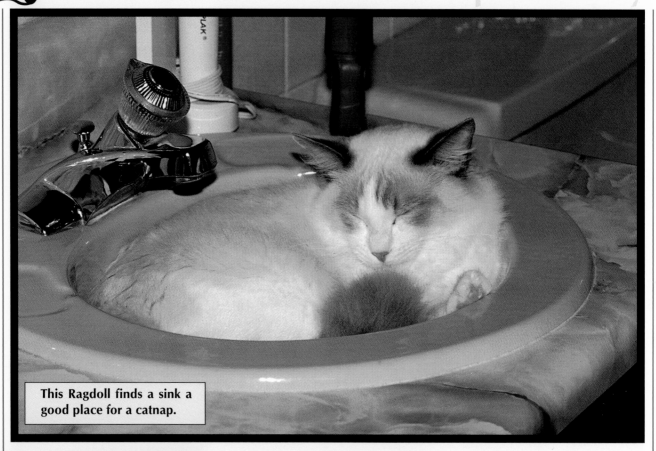

This Ragdoll finds a sink a good place for a catnap.

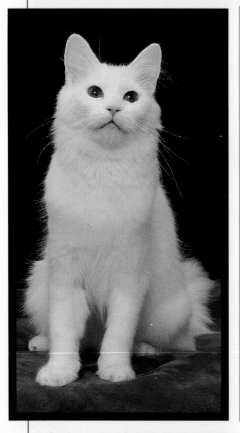

The Turkish Angora, which originated in Ankara, Turkey, is known for its dense, silky coat. It is a progenitor of the present-day Persian. Turkish Angoras come in a number of attractive colors.

Siberian: One of the latest breeds to be introduced to the US, this is a very large cat of the Maine Coon type. It should prove to be both very hardy and popular with those liking big domestic felines.

Somali: This is a longhaired Abyssinian and is a very attractive breed. The longhair gene arose within the Abyssinian and is comparable to the Balinese in its effect. The tail is plume-like, but the body fur is of medium length—-so is easily managed. A well-recommended breed.

Tiffanie: A longhaired Burmese. It has limited US recognition and none in the UK. There are no color restrictions, but it is to be assumed that these will be the same as for the Burmese if the breed is to gain international acceptance.

Turkish Angora: A very elegant and old breed originating in Ankara, Turkey. It is known simply as the Angora in the UK. From crosses between this breed and the Persian, the present-day Persians arose. The fur is dense but silky. Although the original cats were pure white, the breed is seen today in many colors, though in its homeland only pure whites are regarded as being true Angora. It is currently enjoying an upsurge in popularity in both the US and the UK as

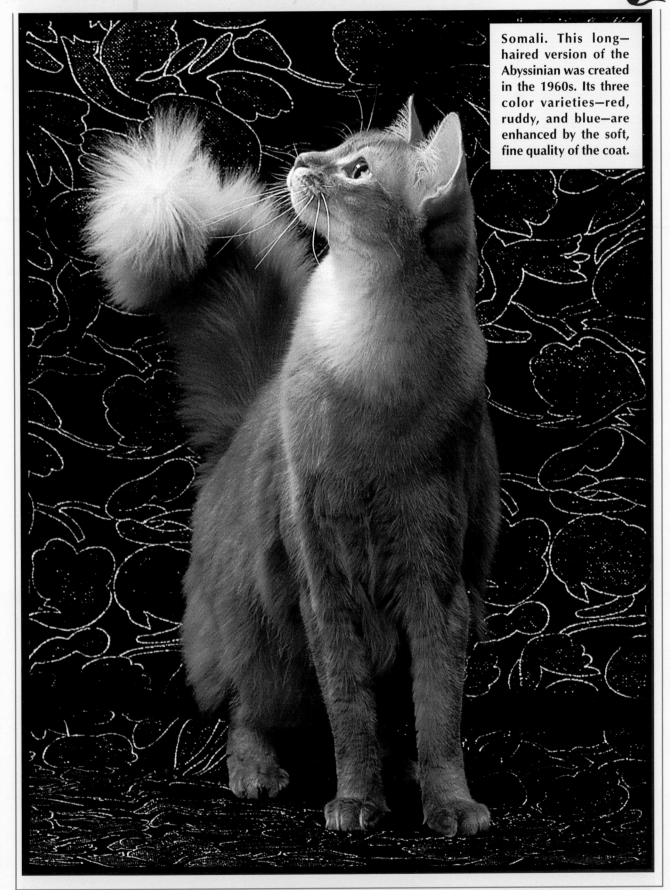

Somali. This long—haired version of the Abyssinian was created in the 1960s. Its three color varieties—red, ruddy, and blue—are enhanced by the soft, fine quality of the coat.

Turkish Van. The coloration of the Van is chalk white, accentuated by auburn markings. Not surprisingly, this breed, which was "discovered" in the Lake Van area of Turkey, is by no means water-shy.

breeders seek those breeds that are essentially unchanged from their original forms.

Turkish Van: This is a regional variety of the Angora but enjoys separate recognition in the UK. Its original color was white with auburn markings on the head and tail, but cream has now been accepted as a color for the markings. Like the Angora, it is very affectionate, enjoys water, and has a more manageable coat than does its cousin.

SHORTHAIRED BREEDS

Abyssinian: This very old breed first gained popularity in England during the 1870s. It was given its present name with the formation of the Abyssinian Cat Club in 1919. It is a noble-looking breed of foreign type that is available in the UK in a number of colors, but only in ruddy, red, blue, and fawn in the US.

The coat has a ticked effect, with the tips of the hairs being darker than the body color. There are also faint

Above: Abyssinian. This breed, which made its way from Abyssinia (now Ethiopia) to England in the 1860s, bears a resemblance to the African wild cat. The Abyssinian's four colors—red, ruddy, blue, and fawn—are enhanced by ticking. Abys are active, social cats that delight their owners with their antics. Below: American Curl, blue and white.

barrings on the legs and tail. A very intelligent feline, the Aby enjoys a select following. It is best suited to homes where its energetic nature is given an outlet.

American Curl: This is one of the newer breeds and is based on a dominant mutation that results in the ears turning outward to a greater or lesser degree. The body is of a soft foreign type. The hair is silky, and a longhaired variant is also in the making.

American Shorthair: This is the classic American equivalent to the very old British Shorthair. It is the regular street cat bred to a high level of quality over many generations. Tough and essentially unaltered over the years, the AS is everyone's idea of what a cat should look like. It is available in a wide range of colors and patterns. Not recognized in the UK.

American Wirehair: This breed is the result of a natural dominant mutation that appeared in 1966 in an American shorthair.

The fur is coarse, dense,

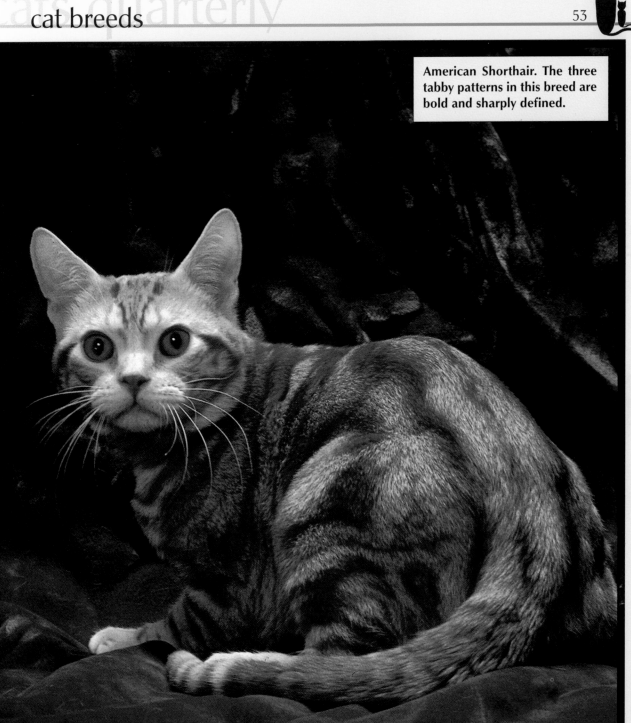

American Shorthair. The three tabby patterns in this breed are bold and sharply defined.

American Wirehair, red and white bi-color. Named for its coat, which is, of course, wiry, the American Wirehair is a cobby and muscular breed of cat.

and hard to the touch, being of a woolly nature. In all other respects, the breed may be regarded as an American shorthair, which is an allowable outcross at this time. Not recognized in the UK.

Bombay: This jet-black breed has a high gloss to its coat. Of foreign type, its development was begun in the 1970s and continues to this day. The parent breeds are the black American Shorthair and the sable Burmese. Of medium size, the Bombay

Bombay. The Bombay's satin-like black-as-coal coat and vivid copper eyes add to its unique appeal.

inherits all of the virtues of the two parent breeds, so it is hardy, intelligent, and very playful. Not recognized in the UK.

British Shorthair: This, in simple terms, is the street cat of Britain refined to a very high standard. Cobby in shape, hardy, and possessing a sleek but dense coat, the British Shorthair, as a purebred, dates back to the late 19th century, when the first cat shows were held. It is available in a wide range of colors and patterns, the

Burmese, sable. This breed, first recognized in 1936, is the result of a mating between a Siamese and a brown Oriental-type female. It is one of the ten most popular cat breeds in the US.

tabby, the spotted, and the blue being especially attractive. Tabby patterns are seen at their best in shorthaired breeds.

Burmese: This breed was established by a carefully planned program that paired Siamese with an import to the US that was of a brown foreign type. The result is a

cat that is lithe and oriental in appearance in the UK but somewhat more muscular in the US. The coat is short and exhibits a high sheen to it. The original color was sable (US), or seal (UK). There are now numerous colors accepted in the UK, but only sable, champagne, (chocolate-UK), blue, and platinum (lilac-UK) in the US. The breed is extremely intelligent and playful, so it is best suited to those who have the time to devote to it.

California Spangled: This breed has limited recognition in the US and none in the UK. It is a spotted breed developed by numerous crosses including the Abyssinian, Malayan

Chartreux. One of the three blue breeds in the fancy, the Chartreux is a robust, well-developed cat with a deep chest and well-developed shoulders. Its coat is medium-short, with just a trace of wooliness to it.

street cats, and others. It is an attractive breed available in a range of colors but is expensive.

Chartreux: The hallmark of this breed is its beautiful blue coat, which is plush and glossy. The tips of the hairs are silver.

The breed is French, though it is thought to carry British Blue bloodlines due to the decimation of the

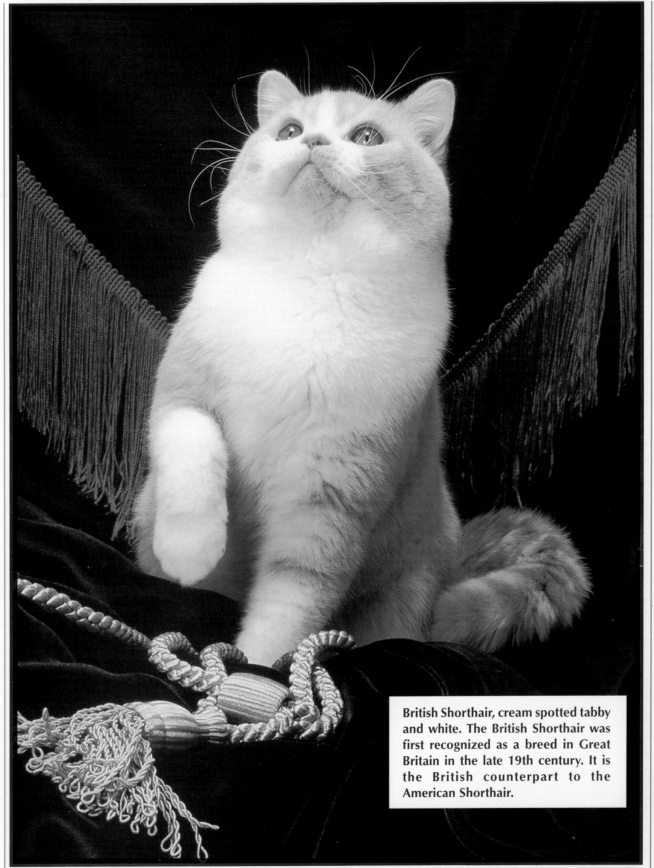

British Shorthair, cream spotted tabby and white. The British Shorthair was first recognized as a breed in Great Britain in the late 19th century. It is the British counterpart to the American Shorthair.

Devon Rex. Like its "cousin," the Cornish Rex, the Devon Rex is a lively, active cat. Grooming—for both of these breeds—requires little more than gentle stroking with a soft cloth.

Colorpoint Shorthair, red point. In essence, this breed is a Siamese with points of any color other than those accepted for the Siamese by most US registries.

Chartreux during World War II. Its stature is that of European Shorthairs, and it has a quiet temperament. As with all blue breeds, it is a very imposing cat.

Colorpoint Shorthair: This breed is recognized by some associations, while being regarded purely as a color variant of the Siamese by others, notably the British. It is a Siamese in colors other than seal, blue, chocolate, or lilac. The additional colors, such as red, cream, tabby, and tortie point, were introduced from other breeds, thus the division over their acceptance as being Siamese. Any other breeds used in transferring color have long been bred out, so the breed can best be regarded as a Siamese.

Cornish and Devon Rexes: These breeds arose from independent mutations that appeared in British pet cats from 1950 to 1960.

The mutations creating the wavy pattern in the fur are at differing locations, which is why they are separate breeds. If they are interbred, only normal-haired cats will result. The fur is soft and curly,

Cornish Rex. The curly coat, which is the result of a mutation, is soft and has a silky texture.

while the conformation is of the foreign type.

Rexes are available in a wide range of colors and are delightful felines that are very striking in appearance. They are not to everyone's taste, however. They should be protected from very cold and damp weather, as their coats are not as resilient as those of normal cats.

Egyptian Mau: If you like spotted cats, then the Mau is one of the breeds you could select from. It is an interesting

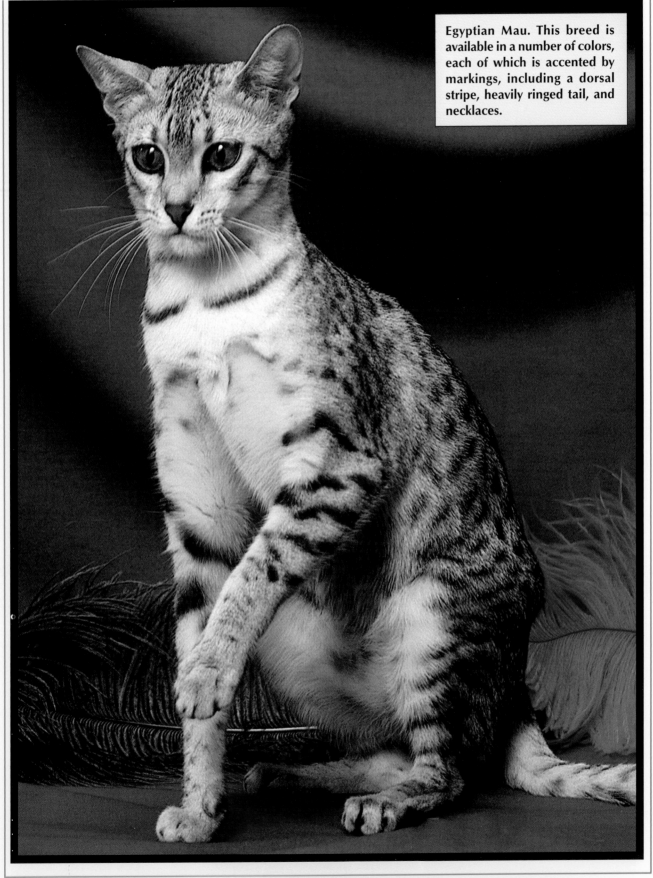

Egyptian Mau. This breed is available in a number of colors, each of which is accented by markings, including a dorsal stripe, heavily ringed tail, and necklaces.

Japanese Bobtail. The bobtail can vary somewhat in length from specimen to specimen. In Japan, the bi-color and tri-color varieties are considered by many to be good luck charms.

Exotic Shorthair: When Persians are crossed with American Shorthairs, the result is the Exotic Shorthair. The object of the original breeders was to produce an American Shorthair that had both a denser fur and a more Persian look to it. The Exotic is a variable breed in its coat quality and is a very well-muscled cat with a short muzzle, giving it a distinctive facial expression: snub nosed. Crosses back to American Shorthairs and Persians are still allowed at this time.

Havana Brown: This breed is known simply as the Havana in the UK, where the breed was first developed during the 1950s. It is the result of crosses between Siamese, British Shorthairs, and Russian Blues. In the UK, the breed is very Siamese in appearance, but in the US it is now more foreign in confor-

Korat. It is believed that the origins of this silver-blue beauty trace back centuries ago in Thailand (formerly Siam). In a good specimen of the breed, the eye color is a vivid shade of green.

Manx, the tailless cat of Britain, the bobtail is not linked to any known abnormal side effects. The breed gained recognition in the US around

breed that was first imported into the US in 1956 from Italy. Its origin is Cairo, Egypt. Its type is broadly foreign, and the quality of its spots are

Havana Brown. This breed, available in a variety of shades of chestnut brown, is the result of a cross between a seal point Siamese and a black Shorthair. Havana fanciers rave about its intelligence and playful personality.

Manx, or Cat of the Isle of Man. The Manx is completely tailless; in fact, there is an actual hollow where the tail would normally begin.

variable. A well-marked individual is most impressive. The colors available are silver, bronze, smoke, and pewter, but dilutions of them are possible to produce blue or lilac for example. Not recognized in the UK.

mation, resembling the Russian Blue in its stature. The color is of course dark brown.

Japanese Bobtail: The short tail is the main feature of this cat of foreign appearance. However, unlike the

1971, though it was evident in the US for many years prior to this.

The colors are numerous, but the bi- and tri-colored examples are those most favored. An interesting breed that has steadily increased its

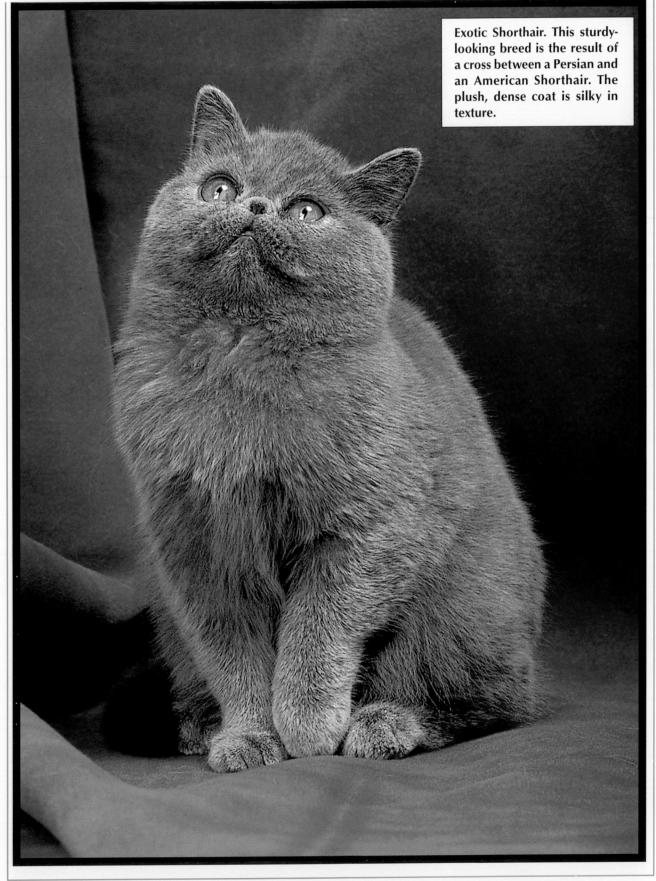

Exotic Shorthair. This sturdy-looking breed is the result of a cross between a Persian and an American Shorthair. The plush, dense coat is silky in texture.

Ocicat, chocolate. The distinctive spotted pattern is the hallmark of this hybrid breed. The Ocicat is named for the ocelot, which it resembles.

numbers over the years.

Korat: This breed hails from Thailand (formerly Siam) and is the third of the blue breeds so far discussed from which you can choose. It is the least well-known of the blue breeds quartet and has a heart-shaped face. However, its popularity has slowly increased in recent years. Its conformation is of foreign type and it makes for a charming pet.

Malayan: In the registries that regard this cat as a breed, it is a Burmese of any color other than sable. It thus has the same build and lively nature as the Burmese. Not recognized in the UK as a separate breed.

Manx: This is the famed tailless cat from the Isle of Man in Great Britain. Not all Manx cats are born tailless, some have tails of variable

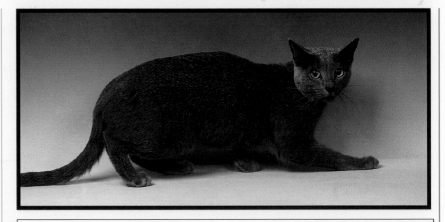

Russian Blue. In some registries, a lighter shade of blue is preferred; in others the darker the blue, the better. Luminous green eyes lend to the Russian Blue's physical appeal.

Oriental Shorthair. This breed is an example of what is known in the fancy as *foreign type*: Slim, long legged, and head tapered into a wedge shape.

length. The tailless mutation is linked to spinal and other abnormalities, so caution is strongly advised before considering this cat. Its conformation resembles that of the British Shorthair, and it is available in a very wide range of colors and coat patterns.

Manx -to-Manx matings result in 25% lethality in the potential offspring.

Ocicat: This recent breed came about purely by chance in an Abyssinian x Siamese litter. The result was so fascinating that a breeding program was begun, and the Ocicat is the result. It is a wild-looking feline with a gorgeous spotted coat that can be seen in a number of colors. It is also quite a big cat, and these facts have made the breed extremely desirable. It makes a delightful pet, but if you choose the Ocicat, watch out for it as it makes a tempting target for cat thieves. It is presently not recognized in the UK.

Oriental Shorthair: This breed, in the US, is a Siamese in any self color, such as blue, red, cream, or chestnut. These would be regarded as Foreign Shorthairs in the UK. In both the UK and the US, the Orientals also include the tabby pattern, the parti-colors, and the shaded colors, such as blue smoke. The breed has the same inquisitive nature and intelligence as the Siamese, of which it can

be regarded as a color variant.

Russian Blue: This gorgeous breed is, of course, blue, and it is the most popular of the breeds of this color. Its body is of a mildly foreign type, and its history dates back for a few centuries. It was one of the first cats to be exhibited when cat shows first came into being in Great Britain during the late 19th century. In the UK, the breed remains lithe in shape; whereas in the US, it is rather more muscular and the face

The Scottish Fold is a unique cat with a bright, sweet temperament.

Siamese littermates, seal point and blue point. In conformation, the Siamese is fine-boned, with slender legs.

more rounded. The coat is short, dense, and very plush.

Scottish Fold: The fold mutation results in the tips of the ears folding forward. This gives the breed its characteristic, and not unpleasant, facial appearance. The mutation occurred in a Scottish cat in 1961. Although the breed has recognition in most countries, its homeland of the UK is not among them.

This is because the mutation, in homozygous form (if both parents of a litter are Fold cats), adversely affects the legs, tail, and spinal column. This being so, Folds should always be mated to normal American or British Shorthairs. The breed is available in a wide range of colors and patterns.

Siamese: This breed is known to people all over the world. It made its Western appearance at the very first cat show in England in 1871. It was improved by the addition of high-quality stock given by the King of Siam (Thailand) to friends in Britain and the US. The Siamese is traditionally seen in four colors: seal, chocolate, blue, and lilac. In its longhaired form, it is known as the Balinese; and in its non-pointed form, it is called either a Foreign Shorthair or an Oriental shorthair.

It is an extremely intelligent feline that is both mischievous and very playful. It is also a cat that uses its voice quite a lot, so will "talk" to you continually. The breed has been used to create many other breeds. Only the Persian enjoys greater popularity. There are many specialist clubs and shows devoted to the Siamese.

Singapura: This is one of the more recent breeds and hails from Singapore. It is a moderately sized cat of foreign type.

Its color is agouti, meaning its fur is ticked. The ground color is ivory, and there are at least two tick bars in a dark brown. There are faint barrings on the tail and legs. Not recognized in the UK.

Snowshoe: This is one of

The Snowshoe is the result of a cross between Siamese and bi-colored American Shorthairs. It is named for the white color pattern on its feet. The Snowshoe is one the newer breeds to emerge in the cat fancy.

the numerous developing breeds in the US. It is produced by crossing bi-colored American Shorthairs with Siamese, then either interbreeding with the offspring, or mating back to Siamese. The objective is to produce a cat of a very loose foreign type that has white paws and points. The latter means the body fur is of a lighter shade than that of the lower legs. The present colors are seal point or blue

The Singapura, which originated in Singapore, received US recognition in 1988. Its coloration is ivory accented by agouti ticking. The coat is short and has a fine texture.

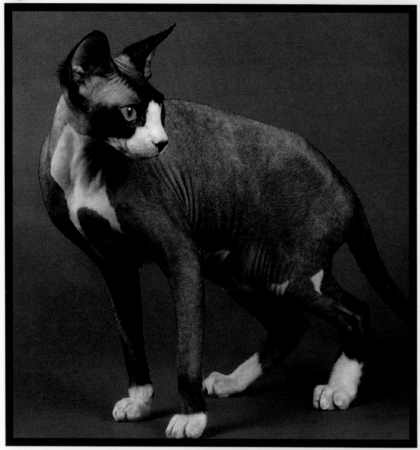

point. In appearance, the breed is somewhat like a Ragdoll or Birman; but it has shorter hair and more white on the body.

Sphynx: This breed is unusual in that it is hairless. Actually, it does have hair, but there is so little of it that it appears bald. It is of foreign type, and the present mutation appeared in Canada in 1966. The breed is not recognized in the UK.

Tonkinese: This breed is the result of crossing a Siamese with a Burmese. It is of a type intermediate between the two and is seen in five colors at this time: natural mink (mid brown), champagne mink (light brown), blue mink, honey mink, and platinum mink (silver gray). It is not recognized in the UK. It is a nice breed for those who like the two parent breeds but would prefer to see a bit more body on them.

For those who seek the truly unusual in a cat, the Sphynx is a top contender. This hairless breed comes in a number of colors and is said to make a devoted companion cat.

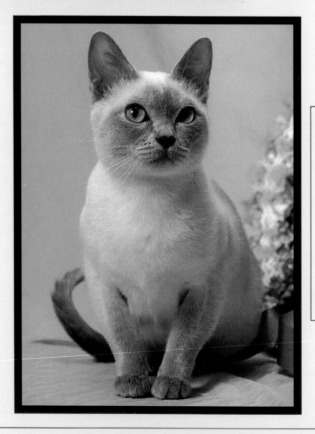

The Tonkinese, a hybrid of Siamese and Burmese origin, is available in various shades of mink. In personality, these medium-sized cats are outgoing and friendly.